G000136009

Shed the consumer of tourism, and discover the real person making her way through Spain. The boringly stage-managed holiday environment is not for her. Instead, she experiences Spain behind the scenes—a Spain peopled with generous eccentricities and fiesta-loving citizens of Europe. On her travels—not plastic funded and traveling in a sixteen-year-old BMW—she finds idyllic and appalling places to stay in and picnics in paradise. This woman relishes a challenge. There are thousands of miles of fascinating description and humorous observations as she takes us to the mountains, the middle, and the Med. The artificial Spain is groomed to pamper the British visitor; the real Spain accepts people for what they are.

AuthorHouse™ UK
1663 Liberty Drive
Bloomington, IN 47403 USA
www.authorhouse.co.uk
Phone: 0800.197.4150

Published by AuthorHouse 11/20/2017

ISBN: 978-1-5462-8472-7 (sc)
ISBN: 978-1-5462-8471-0 (e)

Print information available on the last page.

Any people depicted in stock imagery provided by Thinkstock are models,
and such images are being used for illustrative purposes only.
Certain stock imagery © Thinkstock.

This book is printed on acid-free paper.

Because of the dynamic nature of the Internet, any web addresses or links contained in this book may have changed
since publication and may no longer be valid. The views expressed in this work are solely those of the author and do not
necessarily reflect the views of the publisher, and the publisher hereby disclaims any responsibility for them.

authorHOUSE®

SPANISH SERENDIPITY

A Memoir

CAROLANN MARTYS

Contents

INTRODUCTION

I am not a natural traveller. My star sign is Scorpio and I could live happily under a stone, making the occasional foray for essential needs. I suffer from vertigo and dislike the stress of speed. I don't take kindly to Spanish mountain roads or the Autopista. So what was I doing in the late nineties gypsying around the Iberian Peninsula – my only home a 17 years old BMW?

It was a question of options. As a freelance writer I got tired of papering the toilet walls with rejection slips. I packed laptop, printer, travel kettle, and a large supply of tea bags into the car, crossed the channel and followed the star of serendipity. I was lucky enough to get work writing articles for English language glossies and teaching at an International College. But the brief I set myself was to find areas of rural Spain unexplored by the Brits. By definition this meant following my nose rather than a guide book.

What follows here is a series of adventures that at worst proved to be a smooth guide to rough Spain and at best a transcendental journey into a culture unimaginable from the viewpoint of a Costa deckchair.

The downside? Constant driving, carrying suitcases, once a month mail; unknown language and food; loneliness, isolation. No home, no base, no security. Safer to stay under my stone: get fat, get bored, get old, get a death.

What was out there, anyway? Wilderness, unviolated space; uninterrupted vines, olives, almonds; eagles, nightingales; singing from scaffolds, dancing beyond dawn; nostril-numbing coffee, real bread, rich Riojas; December windfalls of oranges, sweet strawberries in February; strangers speaking, smiling, touching, kissing…

A monumental affirmation of life.

PREFACE

Much of Spain is a disappointing mess, especially on the Mediterranean coastal strip. Manic materialism is not quite the same as the passion for life that the image-makers tell us is the real Spain. This talk about the "Real Spain" is romantic twaddle. The truth is there's a huge gap between reality and the pictures-for-the-public that the image-makers tell us is "real".

Six years of the Iberian experience revealed a few blemishes on the munificent landscape that would be dishonourable to ignore.

The most cancerous blemish is the number of petty criminals, retired Nazis, and working Mafiosi entrenched in the sun. Against that, the other blemishes are relatively benign.

Like the *extranjeros* (foreigner or strangers) who purport to love Spain yet recklessly and happily are responsible for imposing their own cultural environment. There wouldn't be such talk of an imbalance of nationals on Majorca – too many Germans – if there was more regard for local sensibilities. Francis Kilvert wrote in his diary in 1870: "Of all tourists the most vulgar, ill-bred, offensive and loathsome is the British tourist." What would he think now of the Costa ghettos, the bars and restaurants boasting little England without any attempt to translate into Spanish or acknowledge they are in Spain at all?

But stains in Spain can't all be blamed on foreigners. A survey was carried out in the summer of '96 in a major Spanish newspaper. Of the 28 million visitors, 60% valued Spanish hospitality, service, and the quality of food and lodging. On the negative side, top of the list came noise, dirty towns, and lack of ecological care. That same year, Valencia's agriculture councillor, Marie Angeles Ramon-Lin, failed to spend almost a third of a 1,932 million cash grant from the EU. The aid was intended for the fight against soil erosion, creeping desert, and regeneration of land. At the end of the year, 629 million pesetas were returned unspent to the EU.

Corrupt decision-makers are said to be the cause of the devastation of areas through bad or no planning structures. Hillsides speedily succumb to the bacillus of access roads that inexorably produce their common fruit of bright white concrete boxes; over development in the form of high-rises remaining more than half empty for most of the year. The destruction of the very environment treasured by tourists is accelerating rather than slowing down. In Almeria, vegetables that appear in British shops early in the year are grown under hundreds of thousands of acres of plastic – black lakes of synthetic resinous substance. Spain gets the markets but it pays the price.

Mañana is a myth that disappears in an acrid fog of exhaust fumes from cars, vans and motorbikes driven too fast, too close, too impatiently – to service the low paid industry of a relaxing holiday in the sun. Noisy, smelly lorries don't seem to have passed any emission laws, and the hysterical van drivers make British white van man look like a kindly uncle.

For a lot of Spain's natural heritage, the malignant blemish of hunting has already proved terminal. The killing of wildlife in some parts is so rampant that only when there's nothing left worth killing does it stop. On the very first day of the year's hunting season, a brace of protected birds were shot. Friends of the Southern Alicante Marshlands Association reported the death of a pair of *moritos*, a variety of heron so rare that ornithologists have been monitoring the ten pairs remaining in Spain for over ten years. More insidious is the *Caza Cerrada*: fenced in game that can't get away. An outside slaughter house without slaughterhouse restrictions.

The detritus of hunting hits you, like an evil effluence, in car parks, lay-bys, footpaths, and wild open places. Not just spent cartridges but open tin cans, zinc foil, bottles and plastic. Filth is everywhere. It's not just the hunters. There seems to be a national insensitivity to rubbish. Empty bins bear witness to throwing and missing. Picnic sites desecrated by non-biodegradable binges. Plastic bags hung from venerable olive trees. Old mattresses, fridges, bedsteads, thrown over mountainsides. At the municipal dumps, one strong wind blows garbage into vineyards and gardens. Condoms, empty cigarette packs, flies enjoying the remains of sardine tins – unsightly, unhygienic, unsafe.

It seems as if some of the Spanish hate their wilderness – despite the beginnings of green holidays, TV programmes and fixed fine penalties for dumping. It's not an inability to clean up – witness the immaculate beaches and innovative machinery (they've just brought out dispensers of foil covered envelopes for cigarette ends: lazy smokers can leave the envelopes on the beach to be picked up by mechanical collectors too big to collect single buts.) To the Northern European, it's incomprehensible. Maybe the savage ability of drought to effortlessly debilitate is clearer in the national psyche than a benign Mother Nature.

More of a strange growth than a tumour is regionalism. All languages except Castilian were heavily suppressed under Franco. After his death there was a hard won reversal and now Catalan and Valenciano are taught as a first language. Spanish as it is learnt in England and the rest of the world is Casitilian, but Spanish as-it-is-spoke can be any of at least four alternatives. In the north east autonomias of Cataluña, the Mediterranean coast of Valencia and the Balearics about 80% of the indigenous population speaks Catalan plus the local dialect. Road signs in Castilian are sprayed out by activists and the regional equivalent sprayed in. Dictionaries, maps and Guidebooks can become superfluous or infuriatingly cross-referenced. Apart from the inconvenience of trying to find Javea without knowing that it's signed Xabea, or Jalon changes to Xaló, the poor unsuspecting tourist can become dangerously unstuck with the latest batch of single dialect road warnings.

There is a glimmer of hope on the horizon of this isolationism. Recently, the Catalan Supreme Court over-ruled a Cataluñian decree that all Spanish films shown in cinemas in Cataluña should be dubbed in Catalan.

The history of Spain shows a confrontational character. Clearly, it's still around. The topside of all that is an openness, an honesty, an energy, that is refreshing and addictive.

But if I had to choose a place that encapsulates the more enchanting paradoxes of Spain, it would not be the princely Pyrenees, the deserts of Daroca, the garden that is Galicia. It would be a tiny village in the Sierra de Segura, Eastern Andalucia. It's called Hornos.

To assist the reader in putting the following text into perspective in terms of date and time: in the late 1990s, the peseta was approximately 230 to the UK pound.

Reduced hotel accommodation cost can still be obtained at Spanish travel agents by buying tokens (talones) such as Iberchque and Rancotel. Halcon Viajes have travel agencies throughout Spain.

Amigos de Paradores is an organisation run by the Spanish government. It costs nothing to join. You fill in a form and a few weeks later you receive a credit card and a newsletter (in English) with lots of offers at Paradores throughout Spain. There are great deals for the over 55s. You can also get points each time you stay. This means, with careful planning, you can stay half-price and, with enough points, for free. www.parador.es

CHAPTER ONE – GOING UP

VIEW FROM THE HORNOS APARTMENT

I remember a film where an angel went to and from heaven in a hotel lift. If that were the normal mode of transport, I would definitely be living on the next to last stop. My apartment is on the highest building on the second highest mountain village in the largest Natural Park in Spain. The Park is the Sierras de Cazorla, Segora y Las Villas; east of Jaen, Andalucia. The village is Hornos de Segura and I am living at La Luna at the top of Calle San Bartolme.

GOATS

There are five doors in the *calle* (road). Two goats jamming their heads through the open top half, bleating their grievances, share one. Behind another door a stallion stamps on pungent straw. My door is not as grand as the carved wooden door further down the street, guarded by pots of long-limbed carnations, but I bet I have the best view. At night, if the doors are open, the eye can pass –like an art film camera – through the outer and inner doors in a straight line to the terrace where the moon lights up the shadowy lake and olive-groved mountains.

DONKEY LADEN WITH HAY.

My road, like most of the roads in the village, was made by emptying a lorry load of cement over a mountain track. It's picturesquely and painfully uneven. At 2. 00p.m the man next door arrives for his lunch, leading a donkey laden with grass. The donkey's head is so low, his lips kiss the stones. At dusk, the stallion will return with a similar but a different attitude. Meanwhile, the cats rule. Lying, sitting, perching on windowsills, they talk to each other with weird throbbing noises. They seem content but if you go near, they will dart through tiny holes in the wooden doors.

POSTMISTRESS

It took me three days to find the Post Office. I was told it was the last door in my road. There was no sign but by careful vigilance I discover it. It involves walking through a lounge, television blaring, to a small room where the postmistress officiates when she isn't delivering letters around the village - which she does until 12.45p.m. The post goes at 1.00p.m.

It's easier, however, to post a letter in Hornos than to buy fresh produce. For that you must wait until the market arrives on Tuesday. Meanwhile the 500 residents make do with three grocers where they can buy identical tins, packets, crisps, sliced Serrano ham and boxed UHT milk. The *panaderia* (baker) is at the other end of the village. At 11. 00a.m it closes and the remaining bread is piled into a van, which tears around the village hooting loudly at every 20-yard stop.

At least I don't have a problem about drinking the water – which pours its heart out in the tiny plaza at the end of the road. I haven't yet worked out why, when the water's free, all the shops sell bottled still water but not carbonated. It's also strange, even sinister, that there are two banks in the tiny village. They are next door each other and open and close simultaneously. I went into the first one and joined a queue staring through the glass inner door at a recently deserted desk. Moving on to the next bank, I presented my passport and European bank card. After much arguing and many phone calls, I was told it was quite impossible for me to receive any pesetas. I would have to go to the bigger village, six km. of winding mountain road away. Having nothing to lose, I went back to the first bank. The desk is inhabited, the queue dissolved and I was given 40,000 pesetas with a smile and a *buenos dias* (Good morning).

NUN AND PUPPY

FIRST COMMUNION

FIRST COMMUNION

FIRST COMMUNION

One Sunday, I was woken at 8. 00a.m by a loud hammering on the outer door. As the hammering increased the more I ignored it, I threw on a T-shirt and unbolted the doors. In the glaring daylight, a sun-glassed policeman seemed to be telling me something important. As the only word I could understand was *el coche*, I knew it had something to do with my car. I hurried down to the plaza.

Several black-clothed old ladies were sweeping round my solitary car. Others were bringing pots of geraniums. A small table stood expectantly in the middle. It was Corpus Christie. At 1. 00p.m there would be the annual celebration of the first communion. A thick matting of marjoram was spread outside the 16th century village church. After mass, the new communicants dressed like baby brides, sprinkled flower petals in the path of the priest who processed slowly around the narrow streets, stopping to kneel and bless each flower-decked table. A canopy was held over him and the rest of the village followed singing.

I've now become friends with the young policeman who woke me that morning. I'm allowed to use the village council's fax machine free (quite remarkable as faxes in Spain are very expensive) and we have long conversations that neither of us understands. I also have a nightly chat with the nun who sits by the window in her front parlour embroidering by day, but moves her chair outside for the cook of the evening. She has received a special dispensation from her closed Order to look after her dying mother. She has a six-month puppy that constantly evades her but has taken a liking to me. When we catch him, we have a 'chat'. I have so far understood that she loves three things: animals, flowers and music.

The language remains a problem with the strong Andalucian accent. It pays to be careful. For instance, it would be reasonable for me to ask the handsome young policeman to show me which of the houses in the plaza was the town hall. Because of my difficulty in conjugating a sentence, I would normally say *"Ayunmienta?"* with a winning smile.

Fortunately, I looked up town hall in the dictionary first and discovered that *ayunmienta* can also mean sexual intercourse.

On the summer solstice the village had a fiesta. Nobody knew what time it would start. At 11. 00p.m the plaza was deserted except for some tiny boys practising for the world cup with an empty coco-cola can. An automatic tape was yelling *I'm All Shook Up* through giant speakers set up by a wooden platform. Behind me a temporary stand, the length of the square, barmen stand tensing themselves for the rush that was never to happen. As the church bells fought with *Yellow River* to announce midnight, the band appeared. So did a pack of predatorily teenage girls. Slim-hipped, full-lipped, daring the male species with their bare waists and shoulders, they remained impregnable all night behind their giggles.

Nobody danced, except when the band struck up the traditional Spanish dance - the *Pasa Doble*. This had a startling surrealistic effect: People put down their drinks, grabbed a partner, and went into a skilled, sophisticated set of steps. When the music finished, they went back to their pre-PD position as if nothing had happened. The two village bars stayed open until the Sunday sun rose. Workers and students formed a nightlong pilgrimage from the bar in one road, to the plaza, on to the other bar, and back again. At 4. 00a.m the younger men were beginning to roll in time to the alcohol rather than the music. The women remained animated but even further entrenched. Another three hours of downtown Latin American interspersed with tracks from Grease – could I sustain these heights of pleasure? No! On the other hand, as a way of enjoying the Summer Solstice, it's got to be better than hugging some rocks on Salisbury Plain.

Not that one is short of rocks in Hornos. There's evidence of a necropolis dating back to 4,830BC and the castle and fortified walls were built in 1239 after the village was recaptured from the Moors. We have *musulmanas* (muslims) to thank for the impregnable entrance to the village. By car, it's rather like competing at Badminton Horse Trials. After the customary circuitous climb up the mountain, the road caves in at the first sight of houses with a pothole, as wide as the car, into the first cemented ally. As there's no possible way of knowing what's around the corner, it's recommended survival practice to hoot loudly. There are only two 'streets' in the village that can take anything above a mountain bike and only one wide enough for my car. After that it's simply a dented wing and a prayer for a parking place.

Emilio, who manages La Luna, has accompanied me four times on the 45-minute drive to a mountain town which has a garage able to repair the Beema. Emilio likes to practice his English. He was born in Hornos but left at 14 for school and university. He tells me he dislikes village life; that there is less difference between his grandfather and father's generation than between his father and his – because of Franco. He is angry that his mother insists on wearing black. She tells him that she can't break with tradition, that she would be talked about. Why, he asks her, do you worry what people say? Franco is dead. You are only 55, why do you dress like an old woman of 60? I remain discreetly silent.

It's 95 degrees in July most of the day and not much cooler from sunset to dawn. A few times I've been brave enough to take the limping car out of the village for an evening picnic above the lake. The vista is exactly as Jan Morris wrote in her book on Spain:

'The light is brilliant, the colours are vivid, so vivid that sometimes this seems like a painted country as the mauve and purple shadows shift across the hills, as the clouds scud idly across the candlewick landscape of olives and the red soil at your feet seems to smoulder in the heat.'

I park down a track under the shade of the pines and go on a herb and flower collecting stroll. Suddenly, there's a terrific scuffle just ahead of me and a growl as fierce as a lion. I turn around and walk back as quickly and quietly as I can. Looking over my shoulder, I'm grateful that the wild boar is as scared as I am.

There's little else to disturb the peace. The Spanish come up to the mountain villages to walk at weekends. The people here are more Mountain than Spanish. The village goes to sleep at a time the rest of Spain is getting ready to go out. But there's a warmth behind the unsmiling faces and a readiness to talk as I stagger uphill time after time, loaded with shopping or luggage from the car. Struggling against the solid heat, trying to miss the dung and the droppings, I begin to feel like the stone kissing donkey. But when I reach the last door – my door – I know there will be a cool mountain breeze on the terrace, the swifts will be skidding and screaming over a vista that, miraculously, contains not a single pylon, telegraph pole or car. From the balcony, a fig tree falls gracefully down the rocks. The shepherd moves his goats up one rock and down another. Beyond that, the olive trees spread up the mountains, like silent stationary soldiers, to where the sun will set behind the black pines.

Beyond that, I suppose, is heaven.

CHAPTER 2 – IF PIGS COULD FLY

I leave Hornos early one morning in July –my rental is up. The postmistress, her mother, and the donkey owner wave me off. The postmistress's husband worked laboriously the previous evening carrying load after load of my luggage in a rickety wheelbarrow from house to car.

"Come back next year," they yell as I drive off. "Come back in August for the fiesta." Aproned women stop sweeping the street outside their doors to see what all the fuss is about.

FIESTA. CASTELFABIB. RINCON DE ADEMUZ

Parting is a sweet sorrow that travellers can't afford. The road ahead must take precedence. No hardship on this morning's road. It's a particularly fine scenic route, known as *La Toba – Embasala Rio Segura*. Butterflies skim the road for heat – it's impossible not to run them down – white and black, cornflower blue, delicate dove-grey wings on a russet body. I stop for a picnic breakfast and I see wings fluttering faintly on a roadside casualty, but when I look closer it's a corpse being carried off by ants.

The crickets aren't as noisy in the mornings. Sometimes, on evening picnics, one had to shout over the cacophony – like being in a bar with the sound system on high. There's a crane-like bird overhead: long black body and slowly flapping wings. A stork? Easier to identify the Bonelli eagle – a great white thing with black wing-tips. Near the road are clumps of *poléo de menta* which I collected in the evenings to make a delightful savoury mint tea.

I follow the line of the Segura river: mile after mile of sweet country lane decorated with fig trees, wild roses, rhododendrons and waterfalls. Mesmerised, I drive on a solitary path away from the river, climbing up into a wider, parched landscape. In the distance, I see the top of Yeste, a small Bastide town. It's mid-afternoon and the heat is intense. I need to find food, drink and a bed. Taking the line of least resistance, I begin circling the town from the wider outside streets before squeezing my way through the narrow alleys towards the centre. The force is with me: the Yeste hotel has a bar, restaurant and clean reasonably priced rooms. The heat is still raging at bedtime. There's no netting on the windows. Summer night time in rural Spanish hotels is a no-win situation. There is a choice: close the window and have an airless, flyless night or leave it open and enjoy both the air and the flies. I choose no air but get bitten anyway.

This is Spanish walking country and the hotel steps are crowded in the morning with teenagers – their teachers inside enjoying coffee and brandy in the bar. It's early enough to catch the van delivering bread. I make a thermos of hot water with my travel kettle before leaving the bedroom. There's always a socket somewhere in the room, although it often takes fancy footwork to find it and creative flair to keep it plugged into a bathroom mirror light or an overhead television set. In the hot summer days, it's good to get away early and stop later for a picnic breakfast – if one can find a tree for shelter.

I continue on the scenic route. Ayna, a bijou oasis of a place is too near to stop and I aim for the wine-growing area of Requena. It's Sunday lunchtime when I arrive and I anticipate a gourmet meal and a cool siesta. There's only one hotel in town and it appears to have two thousand narrow slippery perpendicular stairs before you even get to Reception. I decide against it and refresh myself with wine and tapa at a packed but air-conditioned Meson in a shady boulevard. I've been told of a place to stay amongst the surrounding villages but get totally lost and end up at Utiel; a town that works hard for its living in the wine industry but has none of the glamour of Requena. At Sunday siesta time only the dust is active. Tired and depressed I wait despondently for someone to direct me to a Hostal. St Nicholas hears me and sends ministering angels – two lovely ladies. *"Sigue!"* they call from their car and I follow them round and through the hot dusty deserted streets, while they jump in and out of their car, looking, sighing, shrugging. At last they find a restaurant that has an adequate room to rent. I go back to move the car but my poor old camel has, for the first time in its seventeen years of life, expired through heat and exhaustion and has to be left to its Monday morning fate.

ALBARACIN

YESTE

I spend most of the night worrying about the car and get up early scouting for garages. There's one very near but when I go back to the car, it starts first go. Such brave loyalty! I promise not to push it too hard. In fact, I can gauge its condition from my own. When I begin to feel too hot and tired, you can bet your bottom dollar that the camel needs a rest and a cool down too. Most of the cars in Spain have windscreen sun-protectors. The first time I burnt my hands on the steering wheel I learnt why. After that it was a question of draping any odd garment over the wheel and gearbox until I could pick up something more adequate. Which I did, surprisingly, in Yeste. The garage was sufficiently customer-free to give me time to gesticulate to the owner what I wanted and for him to scour spider-filled corners, antiquated cardboard boxes and out of reach shelves. We were both thrilled and amazed when he discovered the very thing in the form of a cardboard advertisement. Price?*"nada!"*

CASTELFABIB. RINCON DE ADEMUZ

DOOR IN TOWN CENTRE. ADEMUZ

Now it's time to visit the celebrated Rincón de Ademuz, heading towards Teruel via the tourist honey-pot of Abarracin. Ademuz is described as Spain's tiniest and least significant provincial capital. Of what, I'm not quite sure. For some bizarre reason, it's a Valencian province enclosed within the Autonomia of Aragon. Ademuz is supposed to be worth seeing but I'm not on the American circuit so time and money force me to prioritise.

Besides, it's the spaces between the places that count. I skirt round El Rincón (*the terrace*) of Ademuz through an oasis of valley floor dramatized by surrounding desert rock against blinding blue skies. Then, bypassing Teruel, the road to Albarracin is one huge plateau of golden grain. There's a four-star hotel in Albarracin but the Hotel Arabia, a converted palace below the town, has apartments for the same price as rooms. The stairs are wide and I can park right outside. The large bedroom and even larger main room have balconies enclosed by massive wrought-iron bars. The supermarket is a pleasant walk away by the river and in the opposite direction the climb begins to the town.

At 7.00p.m. the sun blinds the traffic heading up the hill. Stopping my walk to admire the goodies in a shop window, there's an almighty crash behind me. A car – going too fast – has crashed full speed into the back of a parked lorry. The driver gets out unhurt, but half his car is under the lorry. Nobody seems particularly concerned. They shrug their shoulders as the man keeps pointing up at the sun – the apparent culprit. The town is a higgledy piggle of houses painted in pretty colours. Up many higgles and even more piggles, I eventually find the Tourist Office. There's nothing in English.

I want to go and see Mirambel, where Ken Loach shot his thirties drama: *Land and Freedom*. This takes me through the mountains of El Maestrazgo and across the Sierra Sollvientos. It's higher than one kilometre above sea level but it's still hot and I detour to have morning coffee at Cedrillas. A castle ruin flaunts itself above the village, but more unusual is the stump of a massive elm tree in the village square. It was so big it covered the whole plaza but was killed by Dutch elm disease and had to be cut down five years ago.

Now I'm travelling over the highest point – 1655m – of the Southern Maestrazgo. The road is empty as usual. I seem to be driving back into the past: terraces still intact from Roman times, now growing nothing discernible. Suddenly, without warning, the road stops. '*Obras,*' the sign says, Works. Nobody's working but the sign smiles threateningly in the silent landscape, commanding obedience. This means a big detour. The road narrows to a track. It's hard on the camel and even harder on my nerves. I pass an isolated field of enormous black bulls, like black plums dropped from a basket amongst the grass.

The idyllic scenery is spoiled by a pervasive smell of death. There's nothing to account for it, yet it's hauntingly familiar – as if I've lived next to an abattoir all my life. Then I see the giant hoppers on what appears to be deserted farms. No signs; no signs of life; no sight or sound of animals; just a hideous smell of dark death. Teruel, famous for its smoked hams, has been invaded by the pig barons and flooded with intensive pig factories. Only the flies know.

Apparently Ken Loach merely moved a few cars before filming in Mirambel. I can believe it. It has a water font near, which must have been its attraction for passing Romans, Moors and Visigoths. There's nothing else to recommend it once you've squeezed through the ancient stone walls of the village. A hundred years ago, 1000 people lived here; now there are 150. Most of them are playing cards in the bar of the Gonda Guimera – the only place to spend the night. The room is sparse but clean and the beds are cheap and soft but at 3000pts it's still good value. I'm enjoying a pre-dinner soak and listening to the creaking mechanism of the antiquated church bells, which sound like some forgotten, senile Hunchback raising weary arms to strike each laboured chime, when the otherwise silent early evening is shattered by an explosion of sound from a tannoy. There's some words followed by short sharp bursts of music amongst the crackle. Fire? War? Plague? Ah! It's the fruit and vegetable van.

I share dinner with 25 road workers. Theirs was obviously pre-arranged. Unexpected guests fare less well. My *pollo a plancha* (chicken pan-fried on a griddle) is uneatably burnt. I settle for a salad, which consists of tinned peas, rice and carrots. The wine, thankfully, is a good *Rioja*. Upstairs, I close the window and begin killing legions of flies with my shoe. When the road workers come up to their rooms, the familiar slap of shoe on wall can be heard up and down the corridor – and then the snores.

They're all up and out before the flies recommence attack in the morning. I succumb to the Fonda breakfast: masses of coffee and good toast for 230 pts. Then I pass through the bead curtain, squeeze through the dark shadows of the stone wall into the searing light and on to the pig path to Teruel.

There's a massive empty convent in the first town I come to. A nun, out shopping, tells me that a local farmer had bought it cheaply from the church. He wanted to turn it into a pig factory but the whole town petitioned against it and after a long struggle, won. They want it to be a hotel. I hope it will have a vegetarian menu!

I've been to the city of Teruel itself but not actually explored it. Twice, I've braved the tangle of twisted streets. Each time I've been tantalised by glimpses of exotic buildings and interesting exhibitions. Each time I've been unable to find a parking place. If you're not really fit or you worry about the security of your car, then you must be rich enough to stay at the Parador on the outskirts of the city and take taxis.

MAS DEL PI

Whatever I missed in Teruel was well compensated in Valderrobres with the caring hospitality of Ramón and Carmen Salvans who run a farm and Guesthouse outside the town. They would win an accolade from St Gabriel himself. Mas del Pi is down five kilometres of cart track. Ramón grows 11 hectares of almonds, nine of vines – from which he makes his own red, white and sparkling wine plus a liquor called *Madronos Elborci*. He also has 1,130 olive trees; peaches, cherries, hazelnuts and 14 fig trees. Drought has removed some of its paradisiacal lustre – it hasn't rained since last September, eleven months ago. This is a region of climatic extremes: from the coldest winters in Spain to arid temperatures of over 100 degrees. Ramón's almond crop has failed and his olives are sunburnt but he just smiles and shrugs – next year, perhaps, it will be better.

Outside the front door a small steep incline of jutted stones is the remains of a Roman road that started at Valderrobres and circled round to the next town. Mas del Pi's water source was used as a stopover for the night. The present building dates from 1723. There's a cross on the entrance and there appears to be a well extension carved with the date 1877. Inside, it's a Homes and Gardens finca. Electricity is produced through wind-power, so there's not always a light working in the bedroom. There's no choice of menu for dinner (included in the price) but Carmen's cooking is superb and Ramón does a quick change in the wings before reappearing as waiter and butler. This is not a bed and breakfast, it's a home from home. I get up when I want and Carmen, like an indulgent Gran, is waiting with home-made cakes and jam. Come in at lunchtime and there's a salad, cheese and fruit – and, of course, wine. Ramón sees me wandering, orphan–like, in the afternoon and whisks me off in his tin can that passes as a van. I don't know where we're going and I'm none the wiser when we return. I didn't understand a word he said. He kept stopping the van, jumping out and making wild gestures. By the ecstatic expression on his face, it was obviously something worth seeing.

Not many kilometres from Valderrobres is Fuente Spalda. The partly broken wooden doors of its convent were put in place 300 years before Shakespeare was born. The stone carvings above the massive doors are in good condition and the church below the convent has been prettily restored with bright paintings. I fetch the key from the bar next door. By the size of the key, it must be the original. A locked cupboard in the convent reveals a bizarre collection: wax moulds of hands, baby's heads and children's legs. These were symbols given to the nuns for healing prayer. Children's first Communion dresses and faded wedding bouquets complete the eclectic collection.

On the way back to the farm, the smell of pig is at its worst and vultures hover perpetually. Ramón tells me that diseased pigs are left in pits to be burnt but, forgotten, they are eaten by the vultures. More Ramón, less *Jamón*, I say!

CHAPTER THREE – BLACK WINE
AND WHITE MONKS

On an afternoon in August, hot enough for small flying objects to be sautéed on the windscreen, I pull into the garage at Cornudella de Mintsant and ask if there is anywhere to stay. Go and see the hairdresser, I'm told. I catch her opening up after lunch. She takes me to a first-floor apartment. I can have it for 3,500 pts a day. It's basic but bearable. A tiny balcony perches over the narrow street. This is the main route out of town and the noise of tractors, cars and motorbikes is reminiscent of central London. The reason for this manic activity lies in the soil: olives, hazelnuts and vines. My bedroom has no window, which makes it quieter and therefore preferable – if you're not into air and light – except that the flat above is obviously inhabited by a dance troupe dividing its time between rehearsing and running baths. I'm kept awake most of the night, anyway, by the work of a sadistic insect that's left its mark on all unreachable parts of my back.

WASH HOUSE.

One of the reasons I need an apartment is the lack of clean knickers. Three weeks supply, and after that it's a stopover and a washing machine. Four-star hotels have laundry services at prices that would encourage all but the very rich to go knickerless; so the black plastic dustbin liner on the back seat of the car is bulging with socks, tops, shorts and a lot of knickers. There's no machine in the apartment and I'm not into a 12ᵗʰ century washhouse, which is rural Spain's equivalent of a launderette. I go in search of la señora and find her mother is willing and able to do my washing. I carry my own iron and expect my bin liner to be returned with clean, dry but unironed clothes. Instead I am handed a parcel in which every sock is pressed to perfection; each shirt folded and buttoned immaculately, and my sloggies sparkle as new. Gushing gratitude, I ask her how much. 3,500 pts, she beams. What?! I put it down to experience.

As usual, I'm the only English person and as the natives are friendly and familiar, it means long incomprehensible conversations every time I venture forth for an apple or a loaf of bread. They seem to like the idea that I am a writer, a profession easier to convey by mime than, say, a neuro-surgeon. Tonight, surprise, surprise, there's a fiesta. Another chance to stand in the plaza, drinking, gassing and dancing to a seventh rate Latin America band from midnight to breakfast.

A RESTAURANT IN PIEDORALAVES

This is the area of Comarca del Priorat, known as the cathedral of Europe for mountain climbing. The world champion comes here to train. He's probably one of the 400 people who own second homes – there are only 600 all year residents. One of them, Jo, is the hairdresser's English daughter-in-law. She met and married her Spanish husband in London and now helps him run a riding school and restaurant outside the town. Her husband, as deputy mayor, is busy with the fiesta but Jo pops in with a bottle of local Cabernet Sauvignon and some wine talk. The 'black' wine of Priorat, known locally as Tintorera, is thought to have got its appendage from the dark intensity of colour but is now suspected to be because of the Tintorera grape: if you add water to the 'black' wine, it turns grey instead of pink. The new Terra Alta, Tarragona and Priorat wines are undergoing good changes and won't be affordable for the likes of me for much longer.

COOKING OLIVES BY THE ROADSIDE

Two minutes into the centre of the surrounding mountains, vines bake on hillsides too steep for tractors – the grapes are pruned, sprayed and picked by hand. This is a fiesta Saturday in mid-August yet I can picnic, quite alone, on huge white rock outcrops in the company of wild flowers and butterflies without the dust or diesel of passing traffic. In the pretty and isolated hamlet of Escaldei there are a few Spanish tourists sampling wine and wares – honey, sweet nuts, tiny black olives – or wandering round the ruins of its 12ᵗʰ century palace, the first of its kind in the Iberian Peninsula, whose turrets and jutting walls form a bizarre reflection of the mountain under which it stands. The rest of the world is bursting the Costa Brava beaches less than an hour away.

Unless you're picnicking under a local tree, or sipping black wine in a village fonda, the best place to be when temperatures take off is a church. There are two deliciously cool ecclesiastical caverns not too far away. From the road that leads off the motorway, Santa Creus Monastery looks like a small town. On a sunny Sunday, its surrounding restaurants are enjoying good business from the smartly casual Tarragonians and Barcelonese. Perhaps it's the narrow-sloped street that reminds me of a sunny Sunday on Hampstead Hill.

The Monastery itself doesn't open until 3.00p.m. The run up to it through a narrow arch and a totally ignored 'no entry except for authorised vehicles' sign is quiet enough to taste the grandeur of the Royal Monastery. It cost 400 pesetas to go in but I'm early and have the place to myself. I decide against the audio-visual tape in a choice of Castillian or Catalan and go for attunement rather than history. Courtyards of orange trees and moss-covered fountains provide a therapeutic background to the Gothic cloisters, the 16ᵗʰ century kitchen, the 14ᵗʰ century palace and the monk's cemetery. Great wooden doors open the church, which is so long I can barely make out the wall of gold at the end. A coach-load of Tarragonian senior citizens is now glued to the videotape and the vast space is all mine. I try a top C at full volume and hear myself singing round the church for at least three seconds. Just inside the entrance is a stone seat that has been worn down through centuries of being sat on. It's now the shape of 800 years of bums.

I wanted to visit the Monastery at Poblet and booked in for what sounded like a lovely Catalan farmhouse but Masia del Cadet is a disappointment. The advertised swimming pool turns out to be the public pool in the village; they want 500 pts for a TV and there's no 'small bottle of the region's muscatel wine and a local biscuit (carquiñol) on your bedside table'. I had a choice of a small sparse room with no view or a larger room above the kitchen with the air conditioner machine outside the window. However, the Masia served its purpose – which was to enable me to get to Poblet Monastery as soon as it opened in the morning and avoid the crowds.

It's a working monastery, the purchased booklet tells me: 'You have come to visit Poblet attracted, perhaps, by the call of some finely placed stones. Nevertheless, you know something or at least during your visit you have heard mention of the people who live here. But after all' the English translation continues, 'you will wonder "Who are the monks?"' Twenty pages later and I'm still riveted. 'Monk, an ancient word of Greek origin, means "solitary"…but you will ask me, "of what does that life consist?"…his aim is nothing less, to be simply a Christian, but one, I would say, who is a Christian all day long and in all he does. Nevertheless, that following is a pure dream, in view of human weakness, it is a day-lilly, if it is not secured, flanked by some votes which engage it before the Church.'

The gentle monk goes on to describe how a group of 12 monks in white habits crossed the Pyrenees after the Moors had been driven back in 1151 and started a tradition of uninterrupted prayer, work and study until the monastery 'was mercilessly subjected to plunder and complete desecration.' This seems at polarity with my guide book, which states categorically that the monastery was built to unite Aragon and Cataluñia. Burial place of kings, recipient of wealth and favours, decadent and corrupt, it generated hatred and resentment until it was burnt to the ground by local peasants during the Carlist war of 1835. The monastery was restored and repopulated by Italian Cistercians in 1940. I can only assume that they laid the ghost of the "day-lilly" and the new order rose, a more pious phoenix, from the ashes. Unfortunately, the 'orderly ensemble of dead stones' did not 'speak to me of the only thing that counts, love of God and of men' – but the monks' little booklet certainly did.

There were tourists in Prades, 20 quiet woody kilometres from the monastery, but it was market day and I could still park outside the red-stoned village wall. I bought freshly made pizza, washed freshly picked lettuce in the fountain and, with a bottle of Rosado, ate it under a cypress tree further down the road in the ruins of Albarca.

Spain returns to work in the beginning of September. August holiday month is almost over but there's still a frenzy of fiestas in the villages and small towns, as if whipping up to a grand crescendo to finish with a bang not a whimper. I'm already tired and tense when I leave Cornudella at 10.00a.m. Travelling south towards a winter rental but keeping well away from the coast, I arrive at Horta de San Joan. This is where Picasso was born and there's an exhibition of his work but the one Hostal is already full. At the honey-pot of Beceite, in deepest Maestrazgo, there's a fiesta and not a bed to be had. I scout every restaurant and Casa Rurales (B&B) featured in the tourist office brochure to no avail.

I console myself with the knowledge that I am in a learning situation. If you break the ties of the known, you free yourself from the staleness of custom and caution – but you can also end up with egg on your face. You don't know your limits till they are exceeded. It's an occupational hazard for explorers and one that's quickly forgotten when one gets it right as I did at Aliaga in the Parc Geologico. Not far from Valencia, still heading south, I have a main road to myself. I have no idea about the significance of the incredible geographical structures around me and haven't the mental space to find out – it would be in Catalan anyway. The enjoyment lies in the total immersion of the senses. Aliaga could be on the moon for all I know but it has a shop, a bar, a Hostal and no fiesta. There's no one else staying and I picnic on the shabby terrace outside my bedroom in splendid solitude. The evening fades in delicious coolness. I remember the words of the white monk: 'but you will ask "of what does life consist?"' Well, this will do for a start.

CHAPTER FOUR – THE TAIL END OF TWO CITIES

It seemed a good idea at the time. Toledo: one of the most important and influential medieval cities. Capital of Spain until the 16th century; treasure house of the Moors, Christians and Jews who, up to the Inquisition, lived together in peace and productivity; and, of course, Domenico Theotocopoulos – The Greek.

Most of the visitors seem to have made the one hour journey from Madrid. It's the most sensible thing to do – Madrid is probably the nearest parking place. I tried twice to take the car into the old part of town and both times sat for too long in a prolonged hill start position, inhaling exhaust fumes from the car in front whilst trying to ignore the hooting of the car behind. Not a pleasant experience!

The alternative – footing it – is more enjoyable but only if you are able-bodied. Even then, wearing the right shoes is advisable, uneven cobbles cut through thin soles. You can avoid the cobbles by walking close to the walls where a thin strip of polished stone borders the lane but careful balance is essential going down the hill if you are not going to slide in an undignified fashion to the bottom. There's a lot of walking in the old town. Not because of the distances between sites – it's only two kilometres across – but because you have no idea in which direction to walk. It's a bit like an international Treasure Hunt. Little groups can be seen every few yards studying their totally inadequate maps to the chorus of 'Where am I? Where is the cathedral/synagogue/El Greco house?' Anyone lucky enough to find the tourist office joins a long queue, at the end of which one woman stands with exactly the same inadequate map. When it's your turn and you ask the same question as the person in front and behind, she points to a brown blob on the map: 'You are here and' pointing to another brown blob 'here is the cathedral; it's only five minutes' walk, you go left from here.' Great! Except that after the 'go left' you come to a choice of three lanes, none of which are sign posted. Take a wrong one and you can add 15 minutes to the estimated five. So the treasure hunt carries on.

The old quarter has been declared by UNESCO: *Patrimony of Mankind*, possibly because of the controlled hysterical joy and camaraderie when you meet up with up with your fellow hunters at the end. You may miss the treasure altogether unless you make an early start. All the monuments close for the prolonged Spanish lunch. I'm almost trampled on by the herd of visitors being unceremoniously ejected from the cathedral at 1.00p.m. At Santa Maria la Blanca Sinagoga, they take my 150-pts entrance fee and then tell me that I have only five minutes before it closes at 1.45p.m. I thought of hiding in a pew, but there aren't any and it turns out five minutes is enough time to look at the walls, ceiling and floor of a rather small square empty room. Fortunately, I meet the tail end of a group of Americans. 'Over here, over here!' their guide shrieks. 'All those from the American Embassy' glaring at me 'up there on the wall near the ceiling, you will see the only Star of David in the synagogue.' There doesn't seem to be any architectural or other reason for the position but don't dare ask the ferocious guide. He's already yelling: '*my* party, the American Embassy party, quickly now, leave the building.'

Most of these walled wonder towns have little Noddy trains – or as the Mayor of Toledo calls his, *The Imperial Train* – where you can be jostled through the intricate maze of narrow streets, glancing briefly at the celebrated monuments. But you'd miss the ambience of the cafés, the cluttered souvenir stalls and the pastry shops selling light, fluffy marzipan. In Toledo, it doesn't really matter if you miss a monument or two, you can still admire the carving on every front door and catch the spark of sun on the architectural gem of a far-off vaulted window.

There doesn't seem to be much point in staying in the town. My half-price tokens are valid at the Hotel Domenico which sits serenely on a hilltop, sharing with the much more expensive Parador a perfectly balanced vista of spires, domes, river and rock. The Tajo river is the longest in Spain. It's referred to by the tourist info as the 'craggy grief' because the first settlers found it tedious to cross.

From the hotel, it's an easy drive away and upwards from the town through the barely known village of Arges to the silent open rolling hills that seem to be just given away in Spain. This is the Montes de Toledo. Reservoir, granite scenery and ancient olive groves spilling over with wild flowers are not a bad alternative to fighting with 200 hundred overheated tourists for a fleeting glimpse of El Greco's glass-protected *Death and Burial of Count Orgaz*.

The evening is surprisingly quiet in the town, but there are Spanish people dining in the restaurant Asadar Adolfo. Pinched between the giant walls of the cathedral in an old cavern, it's unpretentiously chic. The food comparatively expensive, is not exceptional but the service can't be faulted, particularly the Sommelier, Jose Maria Lopez Querencias. He looks too young for his four year training in Madrid. I choose a La Mancha Gran Reserva 1984. It's so good I ask where it can be bought. Alas! It can't be bought in a shop but he'll let me have a couple of bottles for 1,800pts each instead if the restaurant price of 2,100pts. My salmon smells rather powerful and I wonder if it's off but apparently the source is in the sauce. Jose insists on showing me how it's made. He puts some saffron in a small cafetière and adds water; after a while he adds brown sugar and plunges it. He then pours a tiny coffee cup of the sauce for me to try. It's quite pleasant – if still odd with the fish. Finally, at the end of the meal, Jose Maria gives me a free glass of a truly exquisite raspberry liquor, orders a taxi and, putting his customers on hold, escorts me down the stairs and along the lane to where the taxi has unsuccessfully tried to back up the too narrow cobbles. Looking back, I see him waving. In his long Sommelier apron, the silver tastevin around his neck, against the background of the cathedral, the darkness blurring the edges of modernity, he fades out of the vision like a solitary 19th century ghost.

Taking the small roads around western Madrid in the green and pleasant foothills of the Sierra de Gredos, it's easy but dangerous to become mesmerised by the landscape flashing past the car windows. Mile after mile the road is big and wide, empty, fast. But this is Spain. Suddenly, without warning, the wide road narrows. Incomprehensively I'm weaving through a small cobbled village where juggernauts compete for the pavement like stags with locked antlers. On the other side of the village the wide road continues with a shrug of its snow-capped shoulders.

I'm on my way to Avila – of St Teresa fame, another walled wonder. My taste for the bizarre enjoys learning that Franco kept a mummified hand of St T by his bedside. Whether as a back-scratcher or to please the Bishops one doesn't know. It's now back in its rightful place.

I manage to park by the cathedral and use another half-price token for a night at the Hotel Palacio de Valderrabanos, a former Bishop's palace in the cathedral plaza. I can't use the tokens at the posher Melia Palacio de los Velada, opposite, but can sit undisturbed in its enormous grandiose inner courtyard. The glass roof opens up in summer like a colossal elaborate conservatory.

Avila in March is not tourist infested. Most of the tourists seem to be Italian or American. Parties of French schoolchildren wind through the town like dislocated snakes. There doesn't seem to be a scarcity of locals. If you've ever walked into a room full of people with the expectation of it being empty, you'll know what it's like to be in a Spanish town when the siesta finishes. The tranquil square where I'd sat sunning myself at 3.00p.m. is transformed two hours later into a railway station at rush hour. I buy a box of the celebrated *yemas de Santa Teresa* (egg yolk rolled in orange-flavoured sugar.) They look unappetisingly like eyes.

There's just time to visit a historical honey-pot in the evening. I choose the Royal Monasterio de Sant Thomas Avila for its oriental room. Unfortunately, the room is closed for renovation, which leaves only the cloisters to wander through. The church contains a huge marble sepulchre of Prince Juan, only son of Ferdinand and Isabella who used the Dominican monastery as their summer palace. A sad grey place made more desolate by the garden, yet to be tidied after the winter neglect. The whole monastery seems to reflect the grief left by the early death of little Prince Juan and the untimely departure of the bereft king and queen.

Avila is much smaller than Toledo and lacks its diversity and sophistication. On the other hand, the town is well contained within the walls, making it much easier to get around. Ruled by my slim budget, I can't stay for more than a taster. This is a one-night stand tour. I've taken a liking to St Teresa. At the Convento de la Encarnación, there's a small museum containing her words of wisdom. One surprisingly street-wise reflection on 16th century tourist accommodation is: 'Life is a night in a bad hotel.' What a pity she didn't have half-price tokens for an upgrade and Jose Maria Lopez Quenenicas to look after her.

CHAPTER FIVE – EXTRAMADURA, TO DIE FOR

One morning in 1556, Charles V, Emperor of Spain and half the existent world, crossed the high summits of the Sierra de Gredos in northern Extramadura. Halting the lengthy procession of his retinue – which included his personal watchmaker – he made a solemn vow: 'I shall not cross another pass in my life except that of death.'

The diverse landscapes of granite mountain, fertile valleys, ravines and gorges that captured the attention of the man considered by his contemporaries to be the most powerful on earth, have enchanted every traveller brave enough to wander from the well-beaten tourist tracks. The Greek, Strabo, named it 'the celebrated Elysian Fields, the place for a happy life, the duelling of the gods and the resting place of just men.' It was certainly that for Charles V who, true to his vow, died there at the Monastery of Yuste.

A few kilometres down the road from Yuste, in Jarandilla de la Vera, I find an apartment by literally walking around the town asking – using more sign language than Spanish – in bars and shops. It's in a narrow alley and has a scruffy patio/garden in the back with an enormous fig tree. Surprisingly, it is on the ground floor. Spain is not a disability-friendly country. The exquisite countryside, unspoilt by even hamlet-sprawl, is only interrupted by compact towns and villages. The inhabitants make their living from the land or local industry and live in prosaic flats or terraced houses – mostly shut off from the sun – and with perpendicular stairs and no supporting rail. There are no charming little Gites dotted around, as in France. There seem few options for the poor disabled.

I've arrived just before the May Bank Holiday. In Madrid, the city empties itself and the Madrilenos drive two hours in any direction. The second day of my stay, Florentino, the landlord, turns up (he's head porter at Madrid's second biggest hotel) and starts building a wall right outside my bedroom window at 8.00a.m. each morning. You can't have a Bank Holiday in Spain without a party. The theory behind Jarandilla's is the celebration of the town's patron saint. In practice, it seems to celebrate the invention of gun powder: giant fire crackers are let off at every conceivable hour and place. It could be worse. At nearby El Jarrampias, the villagers throw swedes at a man dressed up in furs and at the feast of El Tarbello in a neighbouring village, the spectators get hit with a rope. The worst, however, has got to be at Villneuva de la Vera, where, they say, donkeys are cruelly mistreated at the notorious *Pero Palo* fiesta. A strange dichotomy in the Elysian Fields!

I escape the fiesta frenzy at Garganta la Olla, a mountain village set in thousands of acres of cherry orchards. I can't find the butcher's shop, still painted the traditional blue of its ancient status as a brothel for Charles V's soldiers. Instead I settle for two kilos of sweet black cherries for 300 pts from a black-garbed granny who weighs them on a portable iron scale that must have been around since the village was built in the 12th century. I wash them in the village fountain that brings pure ice-cold water perpetually from the mountains, and picnic in the sweet silence of the hills.

It's easy to get lost in the old part of Jarandilla. Alleys run in all directions, weaving and interweaving, identified only by a bread shop here, a hairdresser there. A once elegant mansion, bearing the stone-carved date of its 18th century origin, stands alone. Its neighbours fell under the bulldozer and are supplanted by ugly apartment blocks. Wooden planks on outside walls indicate even older houses – most carrying For Sale signs. Some have been sold and beautifully renovated. The mixture of old and new, ugly and elegant are joined together in long terraces like a child's mural.

Crossing between one alley and another, I catch sight of a distant mass of colour: a small plaza enclosed by pretty renovated houses, flowing fountain in the middle and flowers everywhere. Pots of geraniums lining stone steps cascade over balconies; rose trees stand sentry over the fountain and brilliant mauve bougainvillaea scamper up walls. There's even a smart painted bench to sit on and admire it all. A friendly little dog comes up and sits on my foot, obviously accepting me as part of the place. I have no idea where I am and I doubt if I could find it again.

On Sunday morning the locals crowd the town. It's Oxford Street sales crossed with a Buck House garden party. This is First Communion Sunday. At 1.00p.m. the churches disgorge mammas and pappas, uncles, aunts and third cousins twice removed. The pavements vibrate with chatter and clinking glasses. Ten-year-old "brides", angelic in white satin flounces with daisies and white ribbons in their hair, are sucking lollies, enjoying the envy of their younger sisters and the discomfort of their older brothers buttoned up in new shirts.

There seems to be a remarkable difference in the shape of the generations in northern Spain and Extramadura. The third age appear mostly small, squat and square with coarse, slightly Slavic features. The women wear black shapeless garments, and pastel polyester for celebrations. The middle generation has been stretched a little and takes more trouble with its clothes. *Their* children are the new young professionals and altogether different: tall, slim, fashionable – only the imperfect shape of their legs gives a hint of their stock, as if the stretching is not yet completed.

Apart from cherry growing, the main industry of the area is tobacco. Hard to imagine that such a noxious plant could originate in such a pure setting. There are two large factories in the town. Silent and scrupulous, they give no hint of the machinations within. Outside in el campo, abound numerous individual growers. Immaculate fields of red earth where the tobacco plants, looking like innocent lettuces, are planted by hand in neat rows. Alongside, there is always a red brick barn for drying the tobacco. There are no windows, only tiny holes like a battery chicken farm.

Having been in places where the English fear to tread, I thought my Spanish had improved dramatically. It's a precise language that doesn't take kindly to sloppy English mumbling. Fail to enunciate the final vowel when ordering chicken (*pollo*) and you could startle the waiting by asking for a roast penus (*polla*). The catholic natives would not take kindly to referring to the Pope (*El Papa*) as a potato *(la papa)*. I made an enemy for life when I asked one prospective landlady about the size of the pig in her house. The trouble lay as much in my small ability to speak Italian as in my inability to speak Spanish. I pronounced *cocina* (Spanish for kitchen) in Italian *cochina* (Spanish for pig). She was understandably upset.

There is a Parador in Jarandilla. It's a 15th century medieval castle complete with drawbridge, turrets, an arms courtyard and surrounded with olive and orange groves under the benevolent eye of the Gredos mountains. Charles V lived here while waiting for his Des Res at Yuste to be built. Sadly, the restaurant is beyond my budget; instead I go down one warm evening for wine and tapas at a pavement bar. The regional wine, *Pitarra* (too late I discover the word translates as homemade village wine) is atrocious and the tapas selection definitely downmarket. I order what I understand to be spicy chicken wings. *Mollejas de pollo* is actually chicken stomachs. The waiter assures me it's the town's most popular dish. I wonder if they also prefer the stone to the cherry. I don't expect Charles V had any problem with the local food at the Monastery. He probably headhunted the Parador chef. What I need, however, is a long rest with familiar food and I think I know where I can get a good Chinese – 300 miles away on the Costa Blanca.

CHAPTER SIX – COUNTING THE COSTA

There are perfectly sound reasons for driving over 300 miles through wet and wilderness, space and silence; floating on good roads, through extremes of scene and weather to an overcrowded, foreigner-filled resort – apart from getting a good Chinese. There has to be a rest sometime from wet and wilderness, space and silence, from ancient ruins, volcanoes, and desolate prairies; from unfamiliar food, unfathomable languages; from parking on peaks; from perpendicular stairs.

So I'm on the Costa for a comfortable casa. Juanco Guzman, Spanish agent: *"What you want, when you want it"*. There's nothing predatory about Juanco (and yes, it's pronounced Wanco). German and English agents seem to act as if they are doing you a favour by allowing you to rent a villa at a much higher price. Guzzie – as I prefer to call him – has lived in this neck of *los bosques* (the woods) all his life and has the answer to most of the tedious little problems that come with renting. Like when the boiler blew up at the English owned Villa *Lay Oowees* (Lewis). Or the interesting experience of Villa Zaria with its Beverley Hills swimming pool complete with statuary, spectacular views and attractive interior. Two days of bliss and the water ran out. After a further four days of carting buckets from pool to loos, and washing up in bottled water, I moved to more modest accommodation where the owner had paid his bills.

Every villa, inevitably, has things that don't work or don't suit. Spanish owners don't have kettles, toasters or washing-up racks but their houses are homely and less like holiday lets than the English owned. Pictures and kitschy ornaments abound. Northern Europeans own most villas for rent. A German writer owns Villa Ruschke. Pictures on the walls, tapes, videos, books – all in German, of course but a catholic selection from *The Man from Uncle* to a glossy hardback of *Bettlekture fur grosse Goethe-Freunde*. All this culture is slightly marred by the non-functioning of the video player, two loos and most of the lights.

The Costa Blanca expects an annual invasion of 17,000 Japanese senior citizens and 37,000 Russians as well as the traditionally high number of Brits, Germans, Dutch and Scandinavians. Yet renting in low season is still competitive, possibly because of over-development and the dismal lack of central heating – winter in southern Spain can get very cold.

After the picturesque discomforts of El Campo, the accessibility of fresh milk and English newspapers, video libraries, people that speak English – or Castillian – seems less unbecoming. And, at last, a variation of eateries. An excellent Chinese meal knocks me back 900pts, including a reasonable house wine; and a four course plus wine lunch on a terrace overlooking the sea takes 1000pts from my budget.

In Calpe port, the English tend to be lured into restaurants by jolly Spaniards waving jugs of Sangria in the middle of the road. The more expensive Swiss restaurants are popular with the French - and the Swiss. There are the inevitable British bars where Dave, having taken early retirement from the Lancashire club circuit, will entertain you on his synthesiser Wednesday, Friday and Saturday nights. Or the Spanish equivalent: tired salad, *lomo* and chips accompanied by Deidre sweating out a Flamenco dance (and who can blame the girl; she had to make a living after her husband did a flit with a Birmingham bimbo.)

Calpe has at least five more tower blocks than it had two years ago – the price you pay for acquiring marmite in the supermarket. It's good fun discovering new networks. My system is to look for English speaking residents and, smiling sweetly, bring out my list. That's how I discovered Le Bob-Bon in Moraia, where, at the back of the shop, they hire out English videos and will send and receive faxes. It's also the way to find out how to get post. I went to the local Post office to see about renting a *buzon* (post box). I managed to understand that I had to fill in a form and get my passport photocopied. When I returned and queued for another 15 minutes, the guy took the forms, told me they were correct and there wasn't a post box available. So I collected my post from the obliging small supermarket instead.

Benissa and Teulada are unpretentious working towns 20 minutes inland with a predominantly Spanish identity. At Villa Luci in Teulada, I watch swallows dip into the swimming pool and beyond the vines a man is ploughing his field by horse. At night the church tower is a beacon of light over the small town. Before the sun sets and they're slowly absorbed by the night, the mountains are black – as if cut out of paper and placed on an orange and blue picture. Sometimes in the late afternoons, women wander by the sides of the lane outside the villa. They carry shopping bags which they fill with herbs and tiny white snails that grow up the stems of tall weed-like flowers. *'Para comer?'* (for eating?) I ask them. *'Si, muy bien!'* they reply. I never thought the Spanish temperament suited to picking out seeds from pomegranates and flesh from a pebble sized boiled snail.

Teulada is a marble and wood furniture-making town. There are no glitzy shops but the assistants in the supermarket and *panaderia* (bread shop) are friendly and helpful, making shopping a happy learning experience. By contrast, three English ladies closing up the Red Cross shop are grumpy when I ask them about communications with Alicante. 'Haven't a clue – ask at the station.' The railway station is down a small side street at the bottom of the town. It seems no bigger than a shop and has the sleepy look of a finca. Inside, everything gleams in polished stone and is mostly taken up by a bar serving coffee and tapas. At a glass hatch on the wall they sell tickets to Alicante by the Lemon Express – four carriages streaked with yellow that rattle back and forth through the resorts of Denia, Calpe and Benidorm. It takes one hour fifty minutes to Alicante from Teulada, but the scenery more than makes up for the time and the hard-wooden seats.

There's a brand-new *Aula de Cultura* (Culture Centre) in the town with a public library. A small corner contains a selection of English books, presumably donated: Catherine Cookson, Iris Murdock, Reader's Digest compilations and some very old books including John Stuart Mills' book on Utilitarianism. But there's a book I really want to read: Spanish Classic Writers from the Generation of 1898, published by Eyre and Spottiswoode in 1932. There's a fascinating introduction by Henri Barbusse and in the middle of the book I find a small square of purple paper with old fashioned print. It says *Diary Blotter. Ford's Blotting Paper obtainable in 23 colours from all stationers… Always use Ford Gold Medal Blotting Paper.* There's some writing on the back. An assignation? I must try it in a mirror.

Things happen around me and I've no idea why. Today on my walk I passed cars and women going up to the cemetery. I followed the procession of aproned women carrying flowers, stepladders and buckets. The stepladders are for the graves high up on the walls. In Spanish cemeteries the coffins are laid in rows, carefully hidden by marble plaques carrying inscriptions and photographs. Women bustle about, unscrewing the iron surrounds, cleaning and polishing the marble, the brass lettering, arranging flower displays in tall vases – gladioli, chrysanthemums or pretty silk bouquets.

There are a lot of Brits buried here: Betty Smith, Kenneth Downs, Bertie Dodd all died in their sixties. Did retirement in the sun prove too much for stress-clogged arteries? Margaret Robinson was born in Montrose and died 1980 in Moraira. Did nobody know how old she was? Did she die on holiday, unknown and unloved? Poor Stanley Law, 1906-1976, has a completely bare slab but Ronald Griffiths was loved and grieved over when he died aged 64: *Treasured memories of a Beloved Husband and Father. You will always be in our hearts. Loving you always. Doreen and family.* And a nice coloured photo. The English graves are plain and puritan amongst the Spanish plethora of flowers and photos. Unknown stories: who was *Harold Jones "Dark Blue" rests Here*? Rows of memories.

A notice announces that tomorrow, November 1st, is All Saints Day. I can't understand the rest of the notice. It's like losing one of your senses. My lack of Spanish has the same effect as being deaf or blind - I don't know what's going on. I can't communicate. I try to remember the Spanish notice so that I can translate it when I get back to the villa, but on the way I find a dead snake on the road which puts the words right out of my head. The snake seems to be over two feet long but very thin; jet black with beautiful filigree silver threads like a spider's web.

All Saints Day is a Bank Holiday. It seems a good idea to go to Benidorm for the night and join in the festivities. The new stylish four-star Hotel Marina Centre is completely full. They don't take bookings at the hotel, the Receptionist tells me, it has to be done through Thompsons. Down at Playa de Poniente the beach is packed. A smattering of pale pink British bodies, but Benidorm on a Bank Holiday belongs to the Spanish. After a day on the beach, they parade the streets in their finery – from the tiniest tot to the oldest Gran. At 6.00p.m. the bars are as full as at 11.00p.m. I join the queue for a table at the Aragon in the noisiest, happiest, most Spaniard-friendly precinct. Nobody minds waiting; they're all too busy talking. My tapas are brought on a board: smoked salmon pate, air-dried ham, brie, all on thick toast. At 11.30p.m. people are still going into bars and restaurants to eat and drink.

If you set out from Benidorm to find the motorway on All saints Day, don't join any traffic queues. The police are out in full, blowing their whistles and urging you strongly to move on. This can mean that when the cars in front of you eventually stop, you are not at the motorway toll as you thought, but in the municipal cemetery. Because that's where everyone is going. The day is given over to the dead. Not in a mournful way, no one is wearing black and everyone is smiling. It's like a birthday party come Spring-clean for the entire dear departed. And, like the best of Wakes, everyone takes to the bars and restaurants afterwards to party until dawn.

Spain seems to have found a panacea for having the highest unemployment in Europe – one long succession of fiestas. Benissa has a three-week fiesta for St Antonio. The square is taken up with funfair, stalls, barbecues, tombolas – every prize a bottle of wine or a giant ham. 'What's the money for?' I ask a local businessman frying succulent steaks on aromatic coals. 'To fund the next fiesta,' he grins.

For a quieter evening I go to a bar in Benissa and have a glass of wine with tapas of almonds, garlic mushrooms and a beef tasty enough for a dinner party. It cost me 350pts. But forget in-depth conversation: the TV and a pop CD are both playing at full volume; there are *jovenes* (youth) at the snooker table and kids playing round the chairs. Nobody gets drunk, nobody picks a fight. I guess you might say they just love to party.

CHAPTER SEVEN – COSTA CHRISTMAS

Three days before Christmas, I drive out to Orihuela because it has a red square on the map indicating a "monument". The half hour drive from where I'm staying in Cabo Roig starts out well through orange and lemon groves, but as the plantations increase in size so does the shabbiness and an odious smell pervades everything. The large piles of foam by the road may have something to do with it. The smell increases as we near Orihuela.

Seediness encroaches on shabbiness. Tall, ugly sixties-designed buildings cast sinister shadows over tarmac roads. I catch signs of expensive boutiques hiding behind dreary facades like muffled Arab beauties. I see the "ancient monument" high up in the mountains over the valley. I keep driving towards it until I'm off the road and climbing steeply a car-width lane, winding round tight corners, I keep my foot on the accelerator and pray I don't meet an oncoming car. The "monument" is a very imposing building. From the car park, and at that height, the town's shabbiness has not decreased. Rubbish lies over the walls and a smell of urine adds a dimension to the sulphur. It seems like an image of poverty stricken tenements in any large hot town. I can see tiny spaces on rooves with lines of washing, a table and chairs. Dogs tied up, barking; a man scrounging through rubbish on the small spaces not yet built on. Perhaps I'm looking through the eyes of disillusioned tourist scouting for romanticism.

MOUNTAIN MEMORIAL FOR FIRE FIGHTERS

The tips of spires from Orihuela's noble ecclesiastical buildings are no consolation. I take my vertigo and walk with it back down the mountain. I'll collect the car later. The walk down covers the Stages of the Cross but it feels as if the Holy Spirit got buried under the tarmac. The square blocks of concrete with the number of Stages carved on, seem merely small memorials – He was here, but is no longer. I'm surprised at the number of handsome young men walking up and down. Later, I learn that the "monument" is the most famous seminary in Spain and the handsome young men are trainee priests. It's difficult to accept that they can all be asexual or have a sufficiently strong vocation to suppress desire. Perhaps it's a case of "if you don't use it, you lose it."

I cheer myself up with lunch on the way back at a grass-roots hosteleria. There's marked Guadia Civil presence: trophies on the walls and dust covered wine bottles from Franco's time. The tapa is first rate and there's a party going on in the restaurant. This is the office party of office parties. The women sit, stand, scream and hurl bread rolls at each other across a long table at one end of the huge room. The men sit drinking sedately at another long table. The women clink glasses, sing, dance. They see me watching from the doorway and pull me over to join in the dancing. It's all so OTT, it probably wouldn't matter if I cartwheeled naked round the room. They'd eat Germain Greer for breakfast.

The Spanish really do know how to party. There's three weeks of fiestas and nobody seems to run out of steam except me. I've been invited to a Disco for New Year's Eve. At 11.45p.m. three men smoking enormous cigars tell us to go away – the Disco won't open for another half an hour. As they're wearing black trousers and white open necked shirts, I don't know if they're waiters or over-heated guests playing hookey from the upstairs black-tie dinner dance. At 11.55p.m. we only just have time to grab a bottle of *Cava* from the *Barre Libre* (free bar) and open our grapes ready for the Spanish custom of eating a grape with each strike of the clock to bring good luck for each month of the coming year. With the last strike multiple cheek kissing besieges us. This is unfortunate for my escort who has stuffed all the grapes in his mouth without swallowing and now looks like an over-privileged hamster.

There are *bolsas* (bags) waiting for us containing things to wear on faces, heads or wherever the fancy takes you, and things to throw and make noises with. The music seems to be late sixties: *Bye bye Miss American Pie* comes round all evening at regular intervals. The entire dance floor being covered with loose balloons impedes dancing. Slowly, gradually, the place fills up with beautiful people: the men elegant in dinner suits, the women in long dresses slit to the thigh, or short, short skirts. The colour is black and black again. The hair cleverly coiffured, the bodies straight. They laugh, smile, drink, smoke incessantly, and dance, dance, dance. The men take off their jackets, make their ties into bandanas. Now they're all – men and women – dancing everywhere: in the corridors, on the tables, on the bar, moving fluidly, uninhibited, friendly, humorous.

By 3.30a.m. I'm seriously considering a hip replacement and an hour later I crumble, clutching my free pint of Jack Daniels. I don't make it to *chocolates y churos* served at 6.00a.m. At 5. 00a.m.I surrender and leave the beautiful people still partying as if there's no tomorrow. There have been no fights, no vomit – just dancing, dancing, dancing.

New Year's Day is very hot. I get up at 1.00p.m. and zombie around all day. In the evening I drive up to an English bar called B.M's where Sandy told me I could use the telephone for incoming calls. The guy behind the bar looks like a contender for the World Heavyweight Championship. He's never heard of Sandy but, OK, we can use the phone. He's only been here two weeks. The previous owner's wife ran off with someone's husband. The Contender defrosts a bubble and squeak and chips for me – he normally only does English Breakfasts. The clientele is stereotype English abroad: dull, insecure, polite and out of place. There's a toe-curling conversation going on at the bar.

'So, what's new, Trev?'

'Not a lot. Bit rough today.'

'Ad a good night?'

'Yeah, went round to Bill's. Trace took 'er knickers off, danced on the table waving 'em over 'er 'ead. They frew us out at 'af past free.'

'Cos of Trace?'

'Nah! 'cos they wanted to close up and go to bed.'

'Oh! 'ave a drink, Trev?'

'Yeah!'

A mechanical engineer from Stafford who used to sing with a heavy metal band and sports a ponytail, is a relentless fount of information. And I got the phone calls done.

"5 Enerio: A las 18" (5th January at 6.00p.m.) it said on the printed leaflet for the *Cabalgata de Reyes*. Procession of the Three Kings at Torrevieja. I didn't think I would be able to park near the port as the procession was arriving by sea, but there was plenty of room in the large open air car park. It's 6.40p.m. but people crowd the pavements, I obviously haven't missed it. It's got cold so I go inside the Casino and drink brandy and hot chocolate (for 165 pts) sitting on an elegant soft chair. There's a leaflet on the table which shows the route of the procession around the cathedral. There's nowhere remotely near to park, so I wander off to investigate. It's begun to drizzle and the crowds have gone. Only an English couple rowing outside a phone booth over a call they've made to their

son in England who's just received a rollicking from dad for not doing those things he ought to have done (and possibly for doing those things he ought not to have done).

'That wasn't necessary,' says Mum.

'Not necessary?' bellows Dad.

'Well, he did do…'

The words fade as the aggrieved pair wander off to try and enjoy the rest of their evening.

Sure enough, the crowds have arrived around the cathedral. The procession stands waiting to begin; not bored or impatient but chattering, laughing, handing out sweets to the children. Sophisticated floats, tractors, donkeys, horses are lined up. Everyone dressed up and bewigged in nativity and pantomime style. All the roads are closed. Printed signs translate as *"Closed from 3.30p.m. until it's finished."*

It's fun to walk, however slowly. The shops are open and the rain has stopped. I reach the cathedral where, fortuitously, there's a lively bar with tables and chairs on the pavement. I buy a glass of wine and some crisps. Around me mobile vendors sell hot chestnuts, sunflower seeds, sweets, gas-filled balloons that fly high above the magnificently lit cathedral. Loudspeakers are erected on the steps. Jingle Bells in Spanish has a more mystic sound.

It's now 8.00p.m. There's animation as the procession approaches. I fight small children to get to the front and see Mary – a Madonna of a girl – sitting serene on a donkey, clasping her china baby and led by Joseph with a head of artificial curls three times too large. Then comes the first float with a very fat Herod resplendent in gold. Kings and shepherds follow on donkeys, ponies and horses. An enormous lamp takes up one float with Aladdin-dressed young boys running alongside. It's the custom to throw wrapped sweets and confetti; I get quite a knock on the nose from a lemon-flavoured concoction. There's a band between each float, each playing different carols, no synchronisation and no gaps between the floats. But *Once in Royal David's City* mixed with *O Little Town of Bethlehem* and a touch of the *Holly and the Ivy*, stirred and strained into Spanish makes a not too unpleasant experience.

Suddenly it's all over. My untouched glass of wine has been cleared from the table but at those prices it's no hardship. I go up into the cathedral. Like most of Torrevieja, it's new, and lighter than most Spanish churches. At one end is a huge tableau of the Three King's visit to the stable, plus local community and including a Roman fortress. The surrounding statues are crude and unattractive. There are no spaces left for lit candles and, tired, I'm glad to sit in a pew looking over the Woolworth's doll lying naked in a basket at the front of the altar.

As I leave, I give my loose change to the youngish beggar at the door. Crossing the square – all yellow and black ceramic benches; flowerbeds and fountains, as pretty as a posh Powder Room – I look back and see the beggar sitting on the steps lighting a fag. Well, God bless him, and everyone, as Tiny Tim would have said.

Spanish Christmas finishes with a Bank Holiday on January 6th. This is the main present giving day and more of a fiesta than Christmas Day, which is family orientated and where gifts to the children are often in the form of money. Every one of the 17 regions in Spain has its own traditions at Christmas. I was told of a custom that's performed at the end of Christmas Day lunch: children, starting with the eldest, go round the table; members of the family hide peseta notes in their clenched fists; as the child kisses the fist, the fingers fly open revealing the money. But Mama is ever present to whisk the money away for safekeeping.

All the Costa kids are out on the town in Pina de Horadada, on the last night of the Christmas fiesta. Like a lemming, I venture forth towards the cliff edge of Bacchanalia. The only place to eat seems to be a pizzeria: packed, smoky and no foreseeable free table. Loud music and sixteen-year olds spill over from the bars on to the pavements. There are at least three discos with even younger girls and boys. The *jovenes* walk between the bars and discos, linked in pairs and groups. Social sullenness and aggressive confrontation is not groovy in Spain – which makes it more fun for the rest of us.

At 11.00p.m. I drive, desperate with hunger, back on the N332 and whizz up and down looking for eating action. I settle for Don Sandys, full of families to the fifth generation, all having a wonderful time dancing and singing. It's New Year's Eve all over again. Jose Manuel sings and sweats over his synthesiser. They do love their Latin American. Ah here comes a tango. A small, square elderly couple is doing it really well. Their bodies gel together. Moving as one complete unit, they dance all the subtle nuances of their long relationship. Although tomorrow is a working day, the party will go on until dawn. It's one too many for me. Thank God there's eleven months to recover. Or is there?

CHAPTER EIGHT – FROM BENIDORM TO SPAIN IN TEN MINUTES

I'm renting long enough to do some trips. Benidorm is supposed to be the most popular resort in Spain – it's host to over five million visitors a year. It's difficult to see how the resort could offer a more complete holiday: a micro-climate created by sheltering mountains; six km of beach topped up regularly with imported Moroccan sand; a night life that includes over 70 discos; the Benidorm Palace three-hour spectacular show; and even Panchos, off the Playa de Levante starting the evening with a children's clown and ending it in the early hours of the morning with *"Sexy Sticky Vicky."*

What they don't tell you is that only a few miles inland from *Bob and Betty from Barnsley's Benidorm Bar*, there's a Spain that has escaped the massive influx of tourism. The nearest far-away place is Orxeta (pronounced Orchetta), a little village in the heart of a desert valley. Like some bizarre virtual reality, I suddenly find myself in a rocky desert surrounded by a dramatic moonscape of mountains. On one side, the huge cone of Puig Campana pierces the sky, on the other side the opaque water of the L'Amadori reservoir blends into the uncompromising scrub. A few hundred yards further on, a parking place overlooks a different landscape: the plantation of lemons that makes Orexetta the biggest producer of lemons in the Marina Baixa. In the centre of this wide watered valley stands a single peak, pink and beige against an electric blue sky like an icing sugar fairy-tale castle. Around the next corner towering palm trees jostle with giant pines and eucalyptus against a background of even higher peaks.

It's the setting that's unequivocally Spain. I walk from Orxetta's hilltop Hermitage and see nothing but the original rooftops. From here, the village seems to be held in the giant paw of a scaled monster. I feel I could stretch out my hands and touch the living texture of the mountain. The silence is so palpable that I hold my breath in case a sound should wake it.

For a longer trip, I take the Alicante-Madrid N330. Beyond the castle-topped villages – dusty and dirty from the low rainfall, and the stone and marble cutting – I can turn to either Castalia, as green and cool as England's Peak District, or to Fontanares, a prosperous land of wine and grain. Acres of vines and fruit trees give way gradually to pines as the road slithers through the foothills of the Sistema Ibèrico and Penibético to the ancient town of Xátiva. A castle, open to visitors, built by Arabs on a Roman site dominates the town. Walls stretch the width of the horizon. Almost at the castle gates is the Hosteria de Monts Sant, a converted Cistercian monastery. It seems a good place to spend the night but when I settle down with a book in the garden, a terrific series of bangs sends my nerves almost back to England. The sound is like two juggernauts crashing into each other at 80 mph. The church bells start going bananas and I know it's another fiesta. Unable to read, I wander down to the 18ᵗʰ century church. The front rows are filled with chattering women and a few children. The church is deliciously cool after the heat of the day. I sit back and listen as the women begin their rosaries: 'Santa Maria…' fading away again into unintelligible mumble. A soothing mantra!

At 9.00p.m. I'm walking around the walls of the Hosteria in the dark. The castle walls are lit up and the huge parapets look dangerously primeval. A sickle moon hangs above the castle. Any moment I expect Errol Flynn to appear in flowing robes. The restaurant is completely full. Tables are put upstairs and outside but people are still turned away. 11.30p.m. they come in. 12.00a.m. the phone still rings. I go to bed and pretend to sleep. Children are shrieking, everybody's shouting, bells ring, and rockets roar, rave music beats up the town below. Spain may have the highest unemployment in Europe but fiestas can sure take your mind off it.

A late November sun is still blazing the next morning. At 8.30a.m. the beat of the rave music is just audible, the odd rocket lets fly and the bells now call the righteous to Mass. Downhill into town the road lands me at the cathedral where the procession is just beginning. As soon as they are out of sight, a black Estate draws up, the sides covered in huge wreaths, a coffin in the back. The funeral is over quickly and at 1.00p.m. the procession returns and the church fills up with families for the fiesta service. A lull before the storm recommences over Sunday lunch.

On another trip, I turn off the N330 to go through the dry lands of Yecla: a mountain town with an aura of prosperity in the terraced streets that culminate in a towering Arab castle glistening in the quiet siesta sun like a fairy on a Christmas tree. It's a town of contrasts: prosperity from the thriving furniture trade and winemaking, cohabiting with the ghosts of centuries of near starvation. At 4.00p.m. as I arrive, the siesta still prevails. Expensive chic peeps through the metal shutters of closed shops and at the end of a shabby street, a Salon de Té sells pastries at French prices. Sophisticated thirty-somethings gossip over coffee and cake in comfortable chairs – more Sloane Square than rural Spain.

There's a brand-new theatre in the plaza precinct. One large torn poster resists the wind and shows a picture of Niña Pastori wearing little else than a pair of undone jeans. She's singing tonight at 10.30p.m. I queue in the cold when the Box Office – a hole in the wall – opens at 8.00p.m. and pay 2,300pts for a ticket. It's cold in the theatre too but the usher takes me to a seat like the host of a formal party.

The concert starts half an hour late so there's plenty of time to admire the frescoed ceiling, the cream and red décor. The contrasts of Yecla are reflected in the audience: dark squat gypsies, looking as if they've just come down from a mountain encampment, tucked in with the fashionably elegant. Niña Pastori sings flamenco for two hours without an interval. She has two male accompanists and two women who stand and clap but are only allowed one chorus the entire evening.

I stay at the Hotel Avenida, an elegant 18th century styled building on the tree-lined precinct. Inside it's an inelegant hostal with basic rooms overlooking a building site. A final paradox as I leave in the morning are the notices stuck in car windows advertising a state of the art techno *"House"* concert – in English:

"Since 1988 there has been an explosion in dance that has far outlived the expectations of the music industry. The influence of many clubs in London, Birmingham and Manchester has led to the emergence of larger night venues where the House Night Club event was born. Over the recent years garage and house music has become firmly established as the sound of our generation embracing every corner of England and now Two-Faced promotions will introduce House El Principio to the people of Spain and will continue to spread until it has touched all the major cities of the country – Valencia, Barcelona. Madrid… May you all enjoy the new experience 26 October in Jumbo (Yecla). Free Entry."

I haven't been long in Yecla but there's been no sign of Englanders. I wonder what the elderly gentlemen in carpet slippers playing the pinball machine in the cigarette-but strewn bar will make of it.

Leaving Yecla, the almost silent road drops down into Jumilla, famous for its soft strong gulpable wines. Stopping at one of the huge roadside shops I buy 20-year-old wines and *Manchego* cheese. A detour takes me up into the high hills for a picnic at the Monastery of Santa Ana – wonderful walking country. Back on the road towards Archena, desert drama gives way abruptly to the oasis of Ojos – aptly named (Spanish for eyes) . If you blink on the mountain bends you'll miss it.

Well over a thousand years before bull fighting, there were Spas. The Romans introduced their bathing habits to Spain and there are now 87 listed thermal baths throughout the country. Most have their own accommodation and Archena Spa is no exception with three hotels at different star ratings but under the same management. Apparently, they keep busy most of the year with Spanish and Northern European visitors seeking the curative properties of a *balneeario.*

I'm delighted at first with the pretty room at the three-star Hotel Leon. The balcony overlooks an exotic garden of giant palms and orange trees against a mountain background. But it's siesta time – squeezed in between meals and treatments – and the peace is suddenly shattered. Such snorts, coughs, splutters! The TVs are at hearing-impaired decibels, the walls paper-thin. Above, below, on either side – there's no escape. The garden of Eden becomes a prison in hell. I move to the Hotel

Thermaz, built in the Edwardian era, when spas were most popular. Its fin de siecla Mozarabic halls have a welcome solidity.

It's not exactly romantic watching the mostly elderly patients creeping around the complex, looking like maggots in their white hooded bath robes. I haven't eaten but one look at the maggot-filled dining room and I'm in the car and out of the ghetto. Archena plaza is filling up pleasantly. Never before have the superfluity of music, laughter and liveliness been so welcome. The mediocre meal tastes better alongside tables of jovial *Jovenos*. It's Saturday night, there's dancing in the plaza, and chocolate and *churros*. I slink back into barracks before dawn. The smell of sulphur still saturates but the snoring is muted.

If you can't fight 'em, join 'em, as the wise man said. I can't afford a nasopharyngeal nebulization and pharyngeal atomization treatment, so I go for the 20 minute hydro-massage bath. Two flights of stone steps end in a tunnel that appears to be re-cycling air. A short stout woman shouts unintelligibly, pushing me into a dark cubicle with visceral brown and yellow tiles. I'm beginning to feel like Anna Neagle just before the Gestapo ripped out her toenails. There's a huge egg timer on the wall and a tub swirling ferociously with water. Yellow hoses attached to ancient pipes disappear under the water, which grumbles loudly, like an unfed animal, as I get in. I am obviously lunch. When the white sand runs out, I'm released by the reappearance of the jailer and, cocooned in a white bathrobe; I drag my jelly legs back to die quietly in my room. I seem to have turned into a maggot.

CHAPTER NINE – A BLAS FROM THE PASS

GRANDMA HOEING OLIVES

It's the differences not the distances. An hour and a half inland from Alicante airport, sea and sophistication become distant memories as I drive through mountain oases where compact circles of isolated white hamlets dazzle against the blue January sky.

I've come to see the olive harvest. I don't know until I arrive that it's also the fiesta of St Blas – the patron saint of sore throats. As a persecuted Christian in the third century he was on his way to prison when he miraculously cured a small boy who was in agony with a fish bone stuck in his throat. Today the tradition is to share bread, which has been blessed, amongst all the family, including domestic animals, in order to protect everyone from throat ailments during the coming year.

The official saint's day, February 3rd, is next weekend but several villages share the priest so there has to be a Mass and a party in each village on different weekends. I stay with Brian and Pat

Fagg and their two sons, Ben and Tom. They came to the area – known as La Montraña – for a walking holiday. Seriously smitten, they returned to buy an almond and olive farm. When a large terrace house became available in Cuatretondeta, a hamlet at the hub of the local olive industry, they converted it into a delightful Fonda.

It's cheap to buy olive and almond groves here – if you can work it yourself. Most of the 190 villagers are over 80. During the eight-week olive harvest, 84-year-old Juan Moreno works his land six days a week. The secret of his fitness, he tells me, is in the clean air, good climate and pure water that cascades down the mountain into his pipes on its way to the village wash-house and the irrigation pool. There, since farming began in 700AD, landowners have worked a rota to open the sluice gates and water their land.

Prosperity could also have something to do with Juan's longevity. He can make the equivalent of 46,000pts a day during a good olive harvest and that's on top of his State pension – which is higher than the UK – and profit from his almonds. Expenses are minimal too: 11,500pa. rates on a large family house with the same amount going on water.

In late January almond trees encircle the village with a garden of pink blossom. It's warm enough to wear shorts and T-shirt on a walk through the olive and almond trees up to the beginning of the Siguilles of the Serrella mountains, known to the locals as *Los Frailes*, the brothers, because the white pinnacles stare severely down on the village like hermit monks. On top of the Serrella a lookout was posted during the Civil War. On a clear day you can see across to Majorca and Ibiza where Franco deployed Italian bombers. Cuatretondeta was a stronghold of the International Brigade and the first village in Spain to install a telephone – used to alert nearby Alcoy when the bombers were sighted from the mountain. Juan and his friends won't talk about the war; perhaps because the largest building on the village belongs to the Guardia Civil and didn't close until 1993 – eighteen years after Franco's death.

The church is boycotted by most of the elderly men because of its past political affiliation. But at 5.30p.m. every day, the old ladies answer the summons of the bell and sitting in an opulence of blue and gold – as costly and compact as a centrepiece jewel – they say their rosaries aloud. The church bell, like some sort of village control freak, chimes every half hour. For those whose hearing has become impaired through a lifetime of chimes, it chimes each hour twice. Phone calls from the one public box have to be carefully timed – the box is right outside the church.

Back at the Fonda, Brian gives us a fiesta programme. Like all the little hamlets in this region, the local language is not schoolbook Castilian, but Valenciano:

"Verbena Amenitzada per L'Orquesta 'Cuarteto Monte Carlo'" ("a dance enlivened by the Cuarteto Monte Carlo orchestra")

Sounds sort of dignified and sophisticated? That it ain't! A door in the wall opens on to a squatter's nightmare. One large room with whitewash that throws itself at my black coat. There's no heating and the warm day has dissolved into a bitterly cold night. At one end, a small area holds promise of musical instruments. The tiled white floor is covered with dirty paper, cigarette ends, crushed plastic glasses. Up a narrow flight of stairs, there's another room, equally squalid. This was where *"sopar al teleclub per a tots que vuelen"* ("dinner at teleclub for sll those who want it") was held at 21.30a.m. The remains of paper plates, pizzas and quartered oranges lie about looking for a still-life artist. The air is 96% nicotine. On the dirty wall is a poster telling you what drinks you can have at what cost. Beer is cheapest. Whiskey is 400pts. No mention of anything non-alcoholic.

Downstairs the band has started a *pasa doble*. People dance. The youngest is four, the oldest could be 90, (the oldest working man in the village is 97.) Some do it rather well. Ben Fagg is dancing round the floor with a neck-lock on a small boy with glasses. He doesn't seem to be enjoying it as much as Ben. From now on the music deteriorates into sixties stuff – not even in sync. I'm about to give it up as a bad job when a whistle blows and people line up, arms around each other's waists. A slow dramatic march is played. The lines swing from side to side; each group has someone standing in front doing a sort of conductor dance. Some people throw their arms open triumphantly. Am I at a rehearsal for *Carmen*? Or is it something to do with bull fighting? I settle for Christians-Triumphing-Over-Moors.

Whatever, it's the high spot of the evening and I end up leaving at 2.45a.m. Outside, up and down the street, private parties are going on in the cold night air. I know that in spite of – or perhaps because of – the chimes, the monks and the Guardia Civil, they'll party on till breakfast.

Saturday. 10.30a.m. *"Volteig de Campanies I Pasa Carrer Perel Poble A Carrec de la Banda de Gorga."*

The band is on loan from the next village. It marches round and through the narrow streets again and again before retiring for wine and tapas at El Casino, a café/bar that serves as a day care centre for the elderly residents. Just before 13.00p.m. they start up again, arriving at the church headed by three young men and two young women carrying the fiesta cakes on silver platters. The young people run the winter fiesta. With stylish solemnity they lay the plates below the altar for the fiesta mass. The band has presumably gone back to the Casino where there is an imported choir of guitars and singers. My Spanish holds up for the first six words of the 20-minute sermon: 'St Blas was a man who…' two thirds of the way through I catch a reference to 'Marteen Lutter Keeng' – the significance of which is entirely lost on me. There's no wine sipping at the Eucharist. Instead we queue up to kiss the cross held by the priest. Three small acolytes wipe our germs away with a linen napkin. Jeans and trainers show under their white surplices. One of them is the boy with glasses who endured Ben's neck-lock dance. After kissing the cross, we accept a generous slice of St Blas cake and walk out into the sunshine, munching it.

The party continues over lunch at the Fonda but at 7.30p.m. we are in serious mode for the religious procession. The villagers, holding long candles, congregate outside the church. Eight men carry the statue of the saint. The priest follows and then the band, who have transformed their previous rhythms to the deep drama of a single drumbeat and a slow serious oboe. We follow, hugging the walls of the narrow alleys. I notice a plaque on the wall of a house. It commemorates the 100th birthday of Raphael Perez Perez, the Barbera Cartland of Spain. Rich and successful, he lived all his life in the house in which he was born and the village he never left.

At the square, the procession halts. Silence. Everyone is looking ahead down the dark lane. I peer round and am rewarded by an explosion that makes me run for cover behind a group of small children. It's not a Basque terrorist attack but the inevitable firecrackers. A wire hung along the street attached to high velocity firecrackers. One touch of a processional candle and the whole lot go off. There's not much to see other than a mass of light but the pungent smell is quite pleasant as we complete the circle to the church where St Blas is put to rest for another year.

A discotheque is scheduled for midnight but as the guys running it are still eating in our fonda at that time, I decide to give it a miss and go to bed. At 3.45a.m. insistent ringing and banging on the front door wakes me. This goes on for 40 minutes. Eventually there's silence. A short time later, a key turns and there's patter on the stairs. Ben obviously lost – and found – his keys. I think I slept through the five o'clock chime.

It's still dark on Monday morning when Juan sets off to his olive groves. The village is gridlocked with tiny red tractors, like Noddy cars, trying to squeeze past each other. At 6.00p.m. they'll be clogging up the street again, bringing back sacks of olives to be weighed at the co-operative. Ben rushes out at 6.50a.m. to catch the service bus to the Spanish Institute in Alcoy. School doesn't open until 9.30a.m. and he'll have two hours of hanging around.

Soon, he'll have to catch the 5.30a.m. coach to the Spanish Institute in Valencia, where he'll be a weekly boarder- and where he'll only be allowed to speak and write in Valenciano.

I leave the village to the accompaniment of 18 chimes. An hour and a half later, I'm driving in deep traffic through compact piles of tower blocks dazzling against the blue January sky. Cuatretondeta seems a pleasant memory. It's the differences not the distances that count.

CHAPTER TEN – PSST IN PENEDES

There's nothing like local knowledge. Three years ago, hurrying down south on the Autopista, I decided to bypass busy Barcelona and rest up in a village of quiet tranquillity. Another hour of dehydration and diesel poisoning later, I gave up and took the next exit: Sant Sadurni D'Anoia – the world's largest producer of classic sparkling wine.

The fantasy of soaking in a scented bath, sipping cold cava gradually faded as I drove through a place that seemed more like a wine theme park than a town. All roads were marked with dozens of identical signs, each one locating a wine cellar. The biggest suppliers – Friexnet, Cordoniu – sported a potted plant or two, and Cava Blancher supplied barbecue areas for cooking Sunday lunch to accompany their tasty wines. No other concessions were made to public relations, not even a hotel.

The effect of experiencing "champagne" in such unglamorous conditions was like seeing Madonna without her make-up; but in keeping, perhaps, with the history of cava, which was born out of Catalunia's Industrial revolution. The bourgeoisie of the area wanted a local wine to celebrate their triumphs and good fortune during the region's rapid economic expansion. Señor Joseph Reventos, head at the time of the Reventos family who now own Cordorniu, came up with a sparkling wine by Method Champenoise and by 1872 had produced three million bottles.

That Sunday everything was still open for business which made finding a bed more bearable. A bottle of brut Natural later, I found it above a restaurant where lunch was in full swing at 5.00p.m. The tiny scruffy room, three flights up, overlooking a building site, with a bathroom at the end of a torn lino'd corridor, was not welcoming even through a happy haze of cava. For the future it would be No Way, d'Anoia.

Armed with this invaluable local knowledge three year later, but still dehydrated, weary, and south of Barcelona, I drive a further 20 minutes to Villafranca del Penedes and a four-star hotel offering de-lux rooms at less than the price of an English B&B. In fact, August is the time to see the sights of Spain in luxury but on a limited budget. Madrid, Seville, Valencia – the cities and towns are deserted. The Spanish make for the sea or the mountains, leaving behind relatively quiet streets, good hotel deals and uncluttered museums and art galleries. Of course, that may not scratch where you itch – like the railway consultant who, complaining to the hotel receptionist at the dullness of the town, was pointed towards the packed beaches of Sitges.

Just as well he didn't wait for the much-publicised fiesta the following Saturday evening. The usual naff band playing American 60's music and a few exhausted waiters trying to get around the crowded cafés in the tree-lined Rambla. I decide to go Spanish and park on a double yellow line but my race memory keeps popping up pictures of irate policemen and tow ropes. I check up on it every ten minutes. At one point I notice crowds of people standing right by it but when I dash over, it's only a queue for the cinema. Well, how was I to know the films began at midnight? At 11.30p.m. the huge plaza is packed with people walking, sitting, sometimes fanning themselves but always chatting. The highlight of the evening is supposed to be the tasting of local produce: *pan, vino y azucar* (bread, wine and sugar.) This turns out to consist of one stall, every inch covered in flags and leaflets. I join the queue in excited anticipation. I skipped dinner, knowing that in Spain you always get more than you think, hand over 100pts and receive two slices of dry bread thinly sprinkled with wine and sugar. That's it? That's it!

Villafranca is the nearest I've come to civilisation for a quarter of a year and I feel brave – or desperate – enough to get a cut and perm. Making the appointment is easy but explaining what I want is another thing. Nobody in the salon speaks English – they rarely even speak Spanish. There are four different languages spoken in Spain. All languages except Castilian were heavily supressed under Franco, but since his death there's been a strong revival. In most schools and public offices, the local language is compulsory. At least 80% of people in Catalonia, Valencia and the Balearean Islands speak Catalan. Believe me, it's difficult to understand – especially when faced with a hyped-up, enthusiastic lady wielding a large pair of scissors.

It seemed likely that I would end up with a green crew cut. La Señora eventually sends home for her 16-year-old son who is supposed to be learning English at school. There follows a surreal conversation based on vowel distortion and hand movements. 'Coorel?' accompanied by circulating fingers, I understand to mean do I want big or small rollers. I was beginning to feel safe when mamma shouts half and inch from my nose, 'spuma? spuma?' I'm counting the odds against being offered an intravenous injection of a fertility drug, when she returns with a handful of white foam. 'Ah, mousse,' I say. At which they all fall about. Only the English would put a desert on their heads.

After that trauma, it seems safer to stay with wine-speak and I settle down to serious cellar crawls. These range from the sublime to the ridiculous. First planted by the Phoenicians and later expanded by the Romans, vineyards have flourished for thousands of years in the Penedés. The biggest producer is Torres. The same family has run the business since the 17th century but it wasn't until 1870 that the business really took off. Jaime Torres went to America to seek his fortune, which he made in oil and shipping. He returned to Spain to build a state-of-the-art winery. Now the family own hundreds and thousands of acres in Spain, California and Chile. The Penedés vineyard is big enough for English and German speaking guides to bus visitors around. There's also a video show and a rather simple tasting. I don't buy any wine – I've seen the same bottles cheaper in the supermarket.

Shooting back along the road to Villafranca, I spot the Restaurant Jordi, advertising 15 different cavas for 1000pts. I'm not sure which is the sublime and which the ridiculous, but it's a good thing that taxis are cheap and available.

Sunday morning, I drive out to the Nadal vineyard, celebrated for its superb cava. I join the queue – strangely sedate – until we reach the garden. What I took to be prospective tasters turn out to be family and friends paying their respects. The patron went to join the great Sommelier in the sky last night. The vineyard has, understandably, been closed.

In the wine business, tradition has always gone hand in hand with progress but totally organic wines are still a rare commodity. In 1980, Josep Maria Albet I Noya became one of the first wine growers in Spain to back the idea of organically treating the vines and eliminating the use of chemical and synthetic insecticides. Now demand outstrips supply. Antonio, the youngest son of the Duena, is enthusiastic and generous. I taste wines that are out of stock –next year's supply is already sold. They have excellent wines to lay down. Only one problem with that: Beemas don't have cellars.

As a sop to the god of temperance, I take time out for some history. About 10 kilometres from the centre of town, through wall-to-wall vines, is Sant Marty Sarroca with the customary Neolithic/ Roman background. At La Sucarrada, a gravestone from the late Roman Ages was found with Christ's name on it, shortened and written in Greek. No one knows why. A lazy Sunday morning in bed means I'm too late for the Roman church, circa 1204, at the summit – it's just closing for a 1.30p.m. lunch. As is the Santmarti castle with its funeral pre-Romanic monument from the second or third centuries B.C – the only one in Catalonia.

Very hot and thirsty, I decide to compensate with wine and tapas at the first restaurant I come across. This turns out to be Restaurant Ca L'Anna Pepet Teixidor. I don't know why restaurants in rural Spain don't display their parking facilities. This one should have read "half a kilometre up the track, third rock on the left." The fact that the Spanish don't seem to mind makes me presume that the jog to the restaurant is considered an *aperitivo*. Personally, I prefer a dry sherry. On this occasion, with the temperature in the nineties, trying to manoeuvre the car reasonably near to the front door causes both me and the Beema to overheat. But as soon as I walk into the cool, sophisticated interior, I calm down.

There's one unreserved table. When I see the five coloured glass beads on the table instead of flowers, I know it's going to be expensive. The "free" starter (at a cost of 450pts) is a small glass half filled with a cream cheese mixture topped with tiny bits of ice marinated in tomato juice and sprinkled with mint. I shock the elegant waitress by telling her that I'm not hungry (it seems more dignified than telling her I'm poor) and could I order half portions. With her grudging permission I have a transparent *Gazpacho, Els Raviolis de Gambot,* (prawns in the thinnest of pastry packets), a portion of cheese and a glass of *Aueo Muller*, which is a sweet dry wine that tastes like a really good tawny port. The bill, including tax, comes to 4382pts but it's a welcome change from lomo (pork sausage) and chips. I have yet to sample what is described in the tourist information as "the original product raised in the area – a mute duck."

Still hungry for history, I drive the next day to Olerdola, on the road to Sitges. It has been a Des. Res. Since 900B.C but inhabited from the Bronze Age. The Romans, as was their wont, put in mod. cons by carving a massive cistern into the solid rock. Water was collected from the top of the mountain and brought through two channels to a small reservoir, which acted as a filter. You can still walk down the stairway, put in for the cleaners, and stand in what amounted to a water supply of 350,000 litres. A classy touch was added in the 10th century with anthropomorphic tombs. These were carved out of the rock in the shape of the human body. More macabre is the medieval quarter, located outside the walled enclave. Beside the remains of the Romanesque chapel of Santa Maria is one of the most important anthropomorphic burial sites in Catalonia. Its current name *The Pla dels Albats* Quarter, derives from the numerous tombs of new born and very young children buried there.

The best part of strolling around these ancient edifices in the searing sun is the smug satisfaction with which you can now sit in the shade, sipping ice-cold cava at cellar-head prices. Villafranca del Penedes may not have the sophistication of Sitges but nor does it have its crowds. The sparkling wine of San Sadurni d'Anoia is no longer allowed to be known as Method Champenoise but as the more prosaic Metodo Tradicional; yet I bet I can't get as serious a bottle for less than three pounds in France. As they say in Catalunia: 'Picasso wasn't born in France either.'

CHAPTER ELEVEN – PEACH
PATH TO THE PYRENEES

It's a magical journey from the humid wetlands of the Ebro Delta to the Pyrenees via Monzon, Flix and Fraga. The harvested grain fields create a desert where high outcrops of rock tower like discarded pyramids. Abruptly, dryness gives way to plantations of peach, pear and apples. Branches weighed down with ripe peaches almost brush car windows. Along the river Ebro there's green and more green; trees, sunflowers, sweetcorn. A bend in the road and it changes yet again to brown and browner, dry arid dust. No sign of another car. I try not to think about breaking down.

There's a traffic gridlock at Barbastro, north of Lleida, so I wander up to the cathedral. It's situated in a tranquil clean precinct but the cathedral seems strangely soulless. The words come to me:

Sitting in this sacred edifice,

I sent my soul out to find its Saviour.

Unable to find comfort in grey statuary,

It hovered for a moment by a window,

Energising in a stroke of sunlight,

Then soared high up to heaven and

     splat – hit the vaulted roof.

Before leaving, I paid 150pts and lit a candle for this soulless place.

I continue the journey in the early evening, taking the scenic route to avoid the busy Huesca road. The car is dive-bombed by birds the colour of Costa Rica. Fortunately, I don't cross the path of the *quebrantahuesos* (bone breaker), the vulture named after its habit of dropping bones on to rocks to smash them so they can extract the marrow. Forty minutes later, I arrive at Alqezar, one of the prettiest medieval villages in the foothills of the Pyrenees. I park outside a hostal on the hill above the village but are told there are only dormitories. This seemed fun until it was made clear that I would be with the girls. It's impossible to drive in the village so after the customary 28-point turn, I leave the car in the nearest available space outside, and stumble along medieval cobbles to Villa de Alquézar, a charming little hotel. The bedrooms are up two flights as usual, but brand new and tasteful. Breakfast is cold meat, home-baked cakes, and mountain honey in a little glass jug plus yoghurts and biscuits – all included in the room price of 5,500pts.

I decide to stay another night and walk down through the village to a shady panoramic terrace overlooking the valley where I sit sipping wine at a café. Swifts dive within an inch of my head and beneath the terrace sheep stand statue-still with their heads pressed flat against the shaded stone wall for coolness. One shifts slightly into the sunlight but a sharp word from the shepherd sends her scuttling back into position. There's a church near the sheep – Inglesia San Miguels. It's small, unpretentious, and is being restored. I hope they don't scrape away the spirit of the place like at Barbastro.

After making a luggage-laden journey in the early morning rain to the car, I drive through mountain and gorge, via Arcusa, to Ainsa where I book into a hostal to warm up with a big lunch and a siesta. Only to be woken up by the post-siesta stress outside the bedroom window – traffic, road-works, building…El señor accepts my pesetas with an inscrutable expression and I take off again after a quick look at the arcaded Plaza Major in the Old Quarter, where I discover, with astonishment, that I can park.

By now the heavens are black again and, blinded by torrential rain, I drive through a Pyrenean mountain Pass into the eye of the storm. Purple and yellow flashes of lightening streak across the windscreen with simultaneous thunder crashing overhead. Visibility is nil. I think I know what the Egyptian army felt when the Red Sea reverted to normal. Amazingly intact, I arrive at Torla in the Odessa National Park. I'm lucky to get a pleasant room at the Hostal bella-Vista. The village street, which ends at the foot of pine-covered mountains, rivers and waterfalls, is besieged by desolate backpacking hikers, plastic capes clinging to their barelegged sodden bodies. There's no more room at any of the Inns.

The storm rages all night but the morning is bright and sunny. Breakfasting on the pretty terrace, looking up at tree-clad mountains washed with yellow flowers, yesterday's hostile weather seems unbelievable. But I am getting to know the volatile personality of the Pyrenees. Like some beautiful, spoilt princess, her moods can change violently and without warning.

The small hotel was built in 1934 and is redolent of black and white films where people went to stay for the whole summer. A couple from Bilbao come here each year for a month's walking. The rain has spoiled things for them this year. Across the road, outside the Hotel Edelweiss, an English motorcyclist tells me that the main road to Ainsa was flooded the day I arrived. Just as well I came on the scenic route! He's from Whitby in Yorkshire, was in Toledo yesterday and expects to be in the Dordogne tomorrow. Over dinner at the Hotel Edelweiss, I meet a couple in their seventies from Sante Fé, New Mexico. They've been coming here for a month's walking for 30 years, always staying at the same hotel. They fly to Paris, get the TGV to Biarritz and hire a car. They used to come with the late writer, John Masters. Their son from California was with them for two weeks. This is the first time they've been rained off in thirty years.

Two days of rest later, 40km further and 1000m higher brings me to the Balneario de Panticosa. It's been a Spa since Roman times. This Spa is creepy. The run-down Victorian buildings contribute but there's something more. Perhaps it's the culmination of so much sickness or the decadence of a society that "took the waters" for something to do. In the Casino, 1930's paintings as big as walls depict people skiing with a superfluity of health and happiness that's reminiscent of Nazi propaganda posters.

At Panticosa, back down the valley, I think I must have died and gone to heaven. Beautiful tanned men in red coats, white scarves and breeches, ride immaculate horses leisurely around like jewels in the scenic crown of pine covered mountain. Across the river, as noisy as a motorway, the valley falls away to reveal a Show Ring. No need to pay for this three-day event – watch the *Concursos Hipicos En El Pirineo* sitting amongst the Edelweiss!

In the village – one steep street – the church door is slightly open and sweet singing entices me in. It's a sweet church too, unusual in its small grey-walled simplicity. Five women are rehearsing for tomorrow evening's concert. Their voices caress the soft and lilting tune. Cigarettes burn, ignored, between their manicured fingers.

The post box outside the post office is so high on the wall that I have to balance on another wall – the width of my foot – to reach it. Do Pyrenean people have springy feet to bounce up, popping in a letter with each bounce? Or do they ignore this piece of architectural eccentricity and post their letters in the free-standing box at the other end of the village? Mind you, I suppose you could reach it from the saddle.

I wonder if I could interest any of the gorgeous horsemen in a peach-picking party?

CHAPTER TWELVE – NOT A LOT IN OLOT

One hundred kilometres north of Barcelona, half way between the Costa Brava and the Pyrenees is the *Parque Natural de Garrotxa* – the finest volcanic landscape in the Iberian Peninsula. I'm told there are thirty Strombolian volcanic cones, a few explosive craters and over twenty constituted basaltic lava flows. All I can see, however, is a beautiful pastoral landscape of woods, meadows, fields and small villages.

There's also a pleasant town, Banyoles, formed around the Monastery of Sant Esteve, built in 812 by the Benedictine monks who came over with Charlemagne. The best thing about Banyoles is its lake: 175 metres above sea level, the water is constantly renewed and changes colour according to the seasons of the year.

There are immobiliarios in Banyoles but they're hidden in car-shy corners and anything rentable has been snapped up by week-ending Barcelonians. I decide not to waste any more of the day and drive straight to the coast. I've got a half-price token for a hotel in Empuriabrava but first I want to dally in Dali-land, so I take the spectacularly twisty mountain road to Cadaques. *'Muy, muy bonito!'* (very, very beautiful!) everyone says and, surprisingly – considering its fame as the more glamorous version of St Ives – it is. In mid-February, the tourist office considers the whitewashed town to be deserted but I only just manage a parking place. I suppose when the season starts the tourists will have to obey the signed injunction and park on the slopes above the town. The sea is existential blue, the sun is total and there's a narrow road that runs the perimeter of the bay. It also makes me want to paint. High-rise flats and an urban spread into the mountain has not ruined the town. Even the local museum with its vast collection of Dali's surrealistic photographs is unpretentious.

There's a distinct feel of the fifties about Cadaques: pony-tailed girls riding vespers and unshaven arty men sitting outside bars.

Empuriabrava, on the other hand, has all the markings of one of the smarter Costa Brava resorts. My hotel is on one of the many canals that run through the resort. Like Cadaques, it's very quiet now and stillness surrounds the yachts lying like docile dogs in their kennels. I decide to try a short cut to the supermarket: a pleasant walk along the canal – worth carrying the heavy bags of milk, fruit and wine for supper and breakfast in the hotel room. A large yacht glides silently past me and stops at a fuel pump to fill up. The canal is lined with boat-orientated venues – fittings, service, repairs, insurance – such an expensive hobby makes me feel quite frugal. By now the sun has set and the canal, smelling of the sea, has the peaceful aura of a host after the guests have gone home.

Into Figueras, Dali's birthplace, in the morning for more wall to wall parking and immobiliars. The search for accommodation has to take precedence now. No visit, this time round, to Dali's museum in the former town theatre with its bizarre exhibits – including a Cadillac reputed to have belonged to Al Capone that rains in the interior when you put a coin in; and the *Sala de Mae West*, where the sofa makes a picture of her lips.

I drive out of town back towards the Pyrenees on a different route. There's warm sun and the mountain road is dotted with mimosa in full flower. I stop at a hotel on the outskirts of a medieval village, Macanet de Cabrenys. The hotel, Els Cacadores, has the feel of an alpine pension, although it's so near the coast. A wide stream rushes by it. The woods are speckled with violets and mimosa plus the aberration of an enormous floodlit football pitch appearing in the tranquil setting. Back in the hotel, half-trees are burning in the grate but I eat alone that night. Out of season, the hotel only comes to life at weekends when the hunters come and work up an appetite by killing the little that's left of the bird population.

Still travelling hopefully but never arriving, I cross the border, via a tiny Pyrenean Pass, to Roussillon in France and circle back to Spain three days later over the Col d'Ares, making a stop at Molló. There are two hostals, both fairly busy with weekend skiers. I choose the one at the top of a hill by a 12th century Romanesque church. The lane through the village – two ships, a bar and a hairdresser – leads out to the open countryside. Walking past pretty chalets with enviable views, I'm suddenly accosted by two smartly dressed women – one young and attractive, the other middle-aged and fat. The latter starts chatting volubly in Catalan. I don't understand a word but there's something about them that makes me think they're not just visitors asking the way. Now she's pointing to some books in her hand – and the penny drops. Jehovah Witnesses! They speak French and we have a pleasant theological discussion. I ask them where their church is. Half an hour away. How many in the congregation? One hundred. Isn't there a strong Catholic presence in Catalunya? Yes. Doesn't that make things difficult? Perhaps – but people are friendly, they like to talk. Quel surprise!

I sit by the wood fire in the evening. There's a 1983 Torres on the wine list for 724pts. La señora pours the sediment straight into my glass. Discreetly, I empty the dregs from the glass into a six-foot potted rubber plant. I skip dinner and save both money and my over-indulged stomach.

From Molló I drive down the mountain, heading back towards the volcanoes and a charming pension, Mas el Guitart, I've been told about, at La Vall de Bianya. The road narrows. It's grey and misty. Clouds surround mountain peaks like volcanic parks of prehistoric time visible through a sea of smoke. Around a corner, a restaurant sign hangs gloomily outside a building as sombre as the stone church above it. There's a down at heel look that comes after a snow winter but I've had no breakfast and can't be choosy. The front door of Restaurant Sant Salvador de Bianya leads into a dark kitchen. Mine Host and Hostess are busy preparing for a full house Sunday lunch. Could I have a coffee? Yes. Toast? No, only a packet of biscuits. Butter? No way. What about a tortilla? Now you're talking.

I cram myself by an electric radiator in a small dark room. Two budgies keep up an excited flow of chatter while I wait for my freshly made delicious omelette. Afterwards Mine Host allows me to see the dining room. It's the ultimate in rustic mountain gourmet venues. The dark natural stone walls contrast strangely with the comfortable chairs, cut glass and elegant pink tablecloths. Every available space is taken up by his collection of Victorian porcelain dolls, sitting around with painted beaming faces like effigies of sated, satisfied guests. By now firm friends, I'm invited to inspect today's puddings. What a pity I can't stay for the excellent 1400pts lunch. Instead, I'm presented with a list of the dishes of the day – written in Catalan. I could have *Trinxat de muntanya amb rosta* followed by *Platillo de xai a la farigola* and accompanied by *Pa y Vi*. On the way out, I popped into the loo – immaculate and filled with vases of fresh daffodils. *'Volvero!'* I shout over the clatter of pans, 'I'll be back!' I don't suppose they understood.

Mas el Guitart is perfect. The weekenders have gone and I have a choice of the four bedrooms. I choose the Blue room. There's a wild cherry outside the window. Drawn out early by the February sun, it presents its smiling beauty like a young bride amongst its sombre elder sisters of willow and beech. The room is a delightful combination of authenticity and style. Lali Nogareda, our young landlady, was a professional designer; her equally young partner, Toni Herrera, was in television. They opted out of the rat race to renovate an old dairy farm and turn it into a comfortable and stylish Guest House.

One of the reasons I chose this place is that it has a kitchen for the use of guests. Eating out every night is acceptable if you are on holiday but it's not a financial or healthy option long-term. Lali brings me eggs still warm from the hen and I put on my rucksack to walk down the hill to the village shop. It's a perfect Spring day – all very alpine, very Sound of Music. The Pyrenees layered against the blue sky, snowdrops and black granite. Pines bordering the valley of rain-soaked grass; bare-branched trees, streams, and bell-yoked cows too pretty for comfort.

The area shows its Victorian prosperity by the extensive farms dotted around the hills and valleys but the shop is the kind you come across in most rural villages in Spain. Small, dark and crammed with everything you might want – except fresh milk and unseasonable fruit and vegetables. What fresh produce there is looks tired – like withered old women sitting, waiting to die.

There's a bigger village a few kilometres away with a Spa shop that fails to live up to its promising sign. Inside, it's no different than the local shop except for an accumulation of clothes circa 1940. I ask for fresh milk. At the butchers, he tells me, pointing across the road. I buy two escallops and bravely ask for fresh milk. *'Venga'*, and I follow the lady behind the counter, through a kitchen, and a small lounge to a red door that I take to be a fridge. It turns out to be another small room with a huge churn. *'Solo un pico'* – only a little, I gasp, wondering if I was supposed to fill my pockets with the stuff. She pauses a moment and then disappears, returning with an empty Fanta bottle. The reason for this performance is that all milk in Spain goes direct from the dairy farms to factories where it's processed and returned to the consumer tasting little different from the box it's packed in. Back at Lali's, the too pretty cows pass the kitchen window, bells tinkling. I lift a glass of delicious black-market to them. *Gracias, amigas!*

Olot is the main town of the Garrotxa region. Smelly and noisy with industry, there's no trace of exotic history. The medieval town was wiped out by a succession of earthquakes in the 15th century. There are some elegant 18th and 19th century houses amongst the preponderance of banks but there's a shabby grandiose feel to the town.

Not the best place to be stuck, I think, when the car conks out at the traffic lights of a busy junction. But better than the hairpin bend of a mountain Pass. It's a Sunday, which means there's less traffic but no open garages. I put up the red triangle and wander off looking for help.

There are not many people about but I notice that most of them are coming from one direction, carrying full plastic bags and fancily wrapped parcels (the Spanish gift-wrap everything, from a cake to a lipstick.) I walk in the direction they are coming from and discover, tucked into a back street, a shop filled with cooked gourmet delights. It's crowded with people buying their Sunday lunch. We're all into Catalan here so I play safe with a spit-roasted chicken, marinated salmon, some savoury stuffed pastries and a fish-filled red pepper. *Estupendo!* Around another corner I use the same technique of back tracking: up steps, across a precinct of closed Insurance Agents, round another corner – and there it is, another magic shop. Here, everyone's buying fresh bread and cakes. I settle for an almond and pine nut loaf.

Two hours later, I'm in a garage having a new battery fitted. The international RAC had come to my rescue. I'd just finishes my up-market picnic in the car, by the traffic lights, when two guys turned up, charged the battery and rushed off telling me to follow. At a green light they stopped to talk to a man they knew. When the light turned red, they shot off. The battery had died again by then and I had to wait for them to come back and recharge it. When we finally reached the workshop, there was a lot of shouting on the phone and eventually two girls clattered down the stairs from the upstairs flat. Pointing at the girls and the new battery, I was given to understand that I was to be left in the capable hands of 16-year-old Inma and 18 year old Maria. They were indeed capable. As I left the workshop at a time the English gentry would be settling down to tea and cucumber sandwiches, the local Spanish were spilling noisily out of a smart Bistro that no tourist would be able to find. There's not a lot in Olot, but what there is, is good.

Back at El Guitart, I can see an 8th century church from the bedroom window. This is no big deal. There are at least 14 Romanesque churches in the small area of La Vall de Bianya. Between Olot and Banyoles, medieval villages and towns proliferate. My favorite has got to be Besa. It's quiet in the large plaza and hot enough in February to enjoy a coffee at an outside bar before plunging into the cold cavern of the cathedral. I wander off along the cobbled streets to explore the ancient Jewish Quarter and admire the 11th century fortified bridge.

It's siesta time. The heat hardens the silence. The bridge stares at its reflection in the river Fluviá. I'm quite alone, standing on a stone patio where, in the Middle Ages, local Jewish women came to purify themselves in the ritual bathing that took place after their monthly menstruation.

The stillness is suddenly shattered by a piercing insistent shriek. A small lizard runs for cover under a stone and a Griffon vulture overhead sweeps down to investigate the possibility of lunch. As my wounded senses return, I realise the shrieks are coming from my handbag. Quickly I retrieve my mobile phone.

'Hi!' It's my sister phoning from Liverpool. 'You're very clear. Where are you?'

'I'm in the Miqwé – the Jewish Purification baths in Besalŭ, Catalunya.'

'Oh! Well I thought you'd like to know I've just gone through your mail. There are five bills and a bank statement. You're 97p in the black. What d'you want me to do with them?'

I told her as politely as possible.

CHAPTER THIRTEEN - YET ANOTHER COUNTRY

'Laddidee! Laddidee!' The Basque landlady shouted at me hysterically. I didn't know what she was on about. Was she speaking to me in *Euskara*, the 3000-year-old language – or had she forgotten to take her tablets. She grabbed my arm, manhandling me into her sitting room. I was contemplating giving her a sharp blow with my handbag when, still shrieking the esoteric Ladidee! Ladidee! she pointed at the TV. All I could see on the screen was a black car smashed against a wall. The next moment, the screen filled with a portrait of Princess Diana. I looked at my landlady. She nodded furiously: 'Ladidee – meurto!' It was August 31st 1997.

The next day as I continued the journey through Pays Basque, a storm broke with such intensity that the narrow Pass became an enclosed shower room. Out of nowhere a Hostal appeared. I was given lunch of thick bean soup and charcoal-grilled chicken by a tree-burning fire. The newspaper on the scrubbed wooden table spoke of nothing but the death of Princess Diana. Front page coverage was given to the correspondent in Egypt: "Suspicion of assassination," he reported. "Carried out by the British Secret Service,"

I climbed five flights of stairs to wait out the night and the storm in a room of new pine – incongruously modern and comfortable. A documentary of Lady Di's life was on TV. I was glad I couldn't understand the commentary. By losing the sense of hearing, my sight became more acute. I noticed for the first time how much she touched people. Not just a cordial handshake, but a stroke, a caress, a tight long clasp of the hand. Pictures of her alternated with close-ups of family and friends – many of the same age and background. The difference was startling. Diana had a softness, a sweetness, a feminine gentleness, a vulnerability. Spain, like most of the world, mourned a princess who, through her trials, aspirations and intimate persona, became a daughter, a sister, a mother, a best friend. Outside the little pine attic, the rain still battered the skylight, lightning lit up the dark desolation – a fitting Wake for Ladidee.

Seven months later, I'm back – and it's still raining. I want to absorb a little more of the Baztan – the largest area in Navarra – and its 1000-year-old culture. This is the Pyrenees at its most mellow. A landscape described as corrugated paper covered with a green tapestry. Big isolated farmhouses with fields of maize interrupt beech and chestnut woods. I take a turning into the woods to reach the mountain hamlet of Azpilkueta. The road dissolves into a one-car mud track with no passing places. The weather threatens more rain. The tiny road, in poor enough condition, looks as if it may fizzle out around the next bend or over the brow of the next hill and leave me stranded in a bog.

Sometime later, having passed through the valley of the shadow of death, I reach the high celestial fields and look down on Roncesvalles covered in fresh snow. Eagles soar through the mist. The plain of France, towards the western sky, is lit up by bright sun under the leaden sky. Majestic clouds float up to the edge of the mountain where they're lifted up effortlessly, as if by a giant breath. This is the place Richard Ford must have had in mind when he wrote about the Pyrenees 150 years ago: "The scenery…will repay…those who love Nature with their heart, strength and soul, who worship her alike in her shyest retreats, in her wildest forms."

At Azpilkueta and the next hamlet of Elizegui, there are supposed to be *casas rurales* (B&Bs) to rent – but no one is at home. No one to be seen in the pretty flower-smothered, slant-roofed houses. The church is closed. Outside it, I study, uncomprehending, the ancient stone slabs that entomb the likes of *Igarc Ltonea Azca.*

Behind the church, an ugly *Fronton* flaws the picture. The minutest of villages have these pelota courts where the locals play life-threatening games such as *rebote* or *guante.*

Janna Trigoyen Aguerrebere at Casa Eguzkialde in Amaiur has a ground floor apartment available for five days. It's small, clean, comfortable and has a patio for sitting or parking the car – a preferable option to tip-toeing through the debris left by the cows as they walk past. This is "a land of cows" according to the tourist information. I see, hear and smell cows constantly but ask Janna Trigoyen Aguerrebere where you can get some milk and she'll tell you to go to the supermarket at Elizondo and get a box of Long Life.

The farm I'm attached to is just outside the gateway of the village. Amaiue or Maia (signs in Basque country are always in two languages) is one cobbled street of aesthetic delight, which you share with cows, goats, donkeys and dogs. Old timbered houses – as if fallen into crooked repose for their centuries of rest – barns and neat *casas rurales*, crowd together with small-windowed, granite palaces emblazoned with coats of arms – reminders of Baztán nobility. The street ends, as it begins, in a farm but the lane goes up and beyond, past bee-hived haystacks, to an imposing memorial. There are two inscriptions in different languages – neither of which I can understand.

The Basque language, *Euskara*, has nothing to do with any language anyone's ever heard of – except perhaps *Esquimaux*. It's believed to predate the Indo-European languages. Because of its ancient origins, it had to make up modern words. Considered to be the natural bond between the people and their country, it's compulsorily taught in school. In Baztan, Basque is the official language with 80-90% speakers. This makes shopping somewhat difficult, but I have an invaluable list of 36 words in English, French, Spanish and Basque. It reads like this:

English	**French**	**Spanish**	**Basque**
Good morning	Bonjour	Buenos dias	Egun on
Thank you	Merci	Gracias	Mila esker
Supermarket	Epicerie	Supermercardo	Janaridenda
How much is it?	C'est combine?	Cuánto es?	Da?
Sandwich	Sandwich	Bocadillo	Ogitartekoa

At an *Alimentacion (Elikagaiak)* I wanted to buy some Navarra wine – a plausible *vino de Navarra*. How do they expect us to know we have to ask for *Nafarroako ardoak?* A smattering of a Latin language can get you by in most of Spain. In Pays Bazques? Forget it!

Zugarramurdi (pronounced *Zigarramudi*), 40 minutes towards the French border on the Oxtondo Pass is supposed to be a honey-pot. It's actually rather boring – until you reach the caves. I haven't done my homework on the place. Casually reading the French and Spanish notices, it's rather shocking to learn that the giant natural cave was believed to be a centre of witchcraft in the Middle Ages. There's more. Don juan del Valle Alvardo, the Chief Inquisitor, arrested 300 local people (not counting the children), accusing them of holding Black Masses and of being vampires and necrophiliacs, as well as wrecking ships off the Cantabrian coast. On the 7th and 8th of November, 1610, the "sorcerers" received their sentences. 18 were absolved, seven were burnt and five – who had inconveniently died in prison – had their effigies burnt. The rest were given life-sentences. The cave became known as the devil's cathedral and Zugarramurdi, The Village of Sorcerers.

Fortunately for the rest of us, the Inquisition committee and the local Parish Council worked out preventive measures against further infiltration of potential vampires and necrophiliacs. These measures involved salt, mustard, putting laurel branches outside the front door and, if confronted on your doorstep, making the sign of the cross and shouting *'Piityes'*. There's only one teeny problem with all that. If one happens to be unversed in the Basque language, how can one possibly tell if the cacophony of consonants exploding from the pink-eyed possible vampire is indeed a demand for blood. Maybe the guy's just had a late night and is asking for a cup of tea.

The Oxtondo Pass crosses the border where, at St Pée, you can buy tastier Gateau Basque than in Spain. The French police are making their presence felt the day I choose to cross and I get stopped. The Beema is in its customary state of cramness – I don't unpack for a stay under a week. I open the boot and watch their eyes dilate as they take in the mess of suitcases, boxes, books, bottles and toilet rolls (very useful for filling gaps as well as not getting caught short arriving at a rental when the shops are shut.) The back seat carries shopping baskets of food, and black dustbin liners full of clothes to discourage thieves. There is a silent exchange of glances between the two policemen, which I interpret as:

'Have we got to look through this bloody lot?'

'Well, it would certainly take a long time and it's nearly lunch time.'

'Do you think she's the one we're looking for?'

'Dunnow. Ask her some pertinent questions.'

Policeman numero uno turns to me – as usual in this country presuming I speak fluent French – and asks:

'Where have you come from?'

'Spain – I've been on an extended holiday.'

'Where?'

'In the south.'

'Aaah!' a sharp intake of breath between thin twitching lips. 'Marbella?'

'No. Further north – Calpe.'

That does it. The boot's slammed shut. I'm not the Costa del Sol drug runner. I'm not even an ETA terrorist. They won't be late for lunch.

It's a good thing, I think, as I jam my foot down on the accelerator, they didn't ask to see my fangs.

CHAPTER FOURTEEN – LURED OVER THE LINE

After the savage wilderness of Spain – its excitement, its restlessness – France sits on her Pyrenean doorstep smiling and beckoning like a smart bourgeoise Madame eager to relieve you of your pesetas. Quite abruptly, the Pyrenean puertos give way to neat, flower-filled villages humming with self-promotion: posters point to supermarkets, billboards boast the virtues of the village. Every farm invites you to stay – or at least to eat. I'm on the same road, the same mountain, the cows are enjoying the same grass, but crossing the border is like walking off the set of a spaghetti western on to the set of a civilised boutique. For a while it's a relief to know the shops will open at two and you won't have to stay awake to eat dinner at ten. France is so – quiet. Not everyone talks at the same time; there's no constant chorus of builders and bulldozers. And the salads are dressed.

I've been lured across the High Pyrenees for the double treat of Bastille Day and the Tour de France. I drop down to the village of Luchon. Bank Holiday Saturday and it's entirely taken up by a market. I haven't got any francs but through an opening between a fish stall and a carpet seller, I catch sight of a bank with a *distributeur* (ATM) machine. Ignoring a ferocious Frenchman who takes the parking of my car in front of his second-hand furniture stall as a personal insult, I thrust my Visa card into the machine and punch in the pin number. The machine gobbles up my card without a burp of explanation and refuses to regurgitate it. A small hand-written sign in the window informs me that due to the Bank Holiday, the bank will be closed until Tuesday – when I shall be in another place, if not another country.

A few villages further on, I find a bank that's open. They refuse to give me francs on my international banker's card but happily exchange my pesetas at a crippling rate. Carte Bancaire dominates the *distributeurs* in France. From a distance, it's remarkably easy to confuse the small CB square with other credit cards. Any problem and the card is whisked back to England.

A waiter at Auberge D'Herété in Louvie-Juzon tells me where the Tour de France will be passing the next morning. The police close the roads two hours before the race arrives so I have to get up early. There's mounting excitement as I drive near to the race route. Over two hours to go and people are stacked up on the grass verges and along village streets, police worrying them like irritated sheepdogs. Then the police motorcycle escort begins. There's one in front of me; his hand goes out – right, left, beckons, all at fast speed. People are staring as if we're part of the show but, of course, there's no traffic coming the other way so their eyes are at a fixed point. Now the police escort points me off the road. There's a space for one car at the bottom of a farm track. 'No further,' he orders, the road is closed now. 'Can I stay here?' I ask in my perfect French. 'Yes!' A perfect place, inches from the race.

It's dark now, spitting, foggy, and threatening as only the power-freak Pyrenees can be. The TV helicopters pass optimistically overhead. I'm thankful for my flask of hot coffee. A woman and two children wander down the farm track. Then a cowherd appears in beret, smock, and stick – straight out of an advert. He's left his cows in the field; there doesn't seem to be anything to prevent them from wandering on to the road. It's going to be a long cold wait. But I didn't know about the circus parade. With a fanfare of car hooters, the fun propels into view – police, press, promotions. A giant Michelin Man sways round the bend. Lorries, vans, cars with sophisticated sculptures scurry past. Packets of coffee, sweets and nuts are thrown out haphazardly, but the children are too quick for me. I look at them threateningly and they hand me a minute *Champion* flag to wave. By the time the cyclists arrive it's pouring with rain. The pack is small, bunched up on the narrow road – it seems half the size it should be. Wait! Let me at least take a photo. It's over. Just one big orgasmic build-up and then – as the French say – pouf! Only a little after play, with the bright yellow support cars carrying spare bikes and Mavic cycle parts. And an ambulance. The parade dwindles out and I'm left with a wet, empty road. Still, I've seen the Tour de France!

Bastille Day: rain prevents play. No fireworks, not even a damp squib. Seems the right mood for repentance so I journey on to Lourdes – and nearly miss the bijou buildings of Betharram. Sunshine peeping through the trees of the sweet downward sloping lane picks out a monument in the wood. The lane opens out into a dream of silent grey, black and white buildings: elegant chateaux, squeaky-clean bridges, and at the centre, the church that sold Bernadette Soubirous her first Rosary. Before Lourdes, there was Betharram. Before St Bernadette's apparition at the grotto in Lourdes, there were centuries of miracles at Betharram.

In 1616, a huge cross was erected on the hilltop above the church. Two months later, it was struck by a storm and then rerercted itself, enveloped by a radiant light. The Archbishop of Paris described 82 miracles between 1620 and 1642. Yet who has heard of the place that, according to St Vincent de Paul, was the second greatest pilgrimage centre of the kingdom of France?

The monument that guided me to this startling town is one of 15 Stations of the Cross. They climb up a woody hill that's more of a hike than a meditative meander. Saint Michael Garicoits had them built. He was St Bernadette's Confessor and the only person to believe from the start in the apparition. When warned that Lourdes would overshadow Betharram, he replied, 'what does it matter if Our Lady is honoured?' I think this guy, and this place, deserve acknowledgement. Like the Indian pilgrims who roll their way to Mecca, greater love hath no woman than to climb 15 Stations of the Cross in unsuitable shoes.

The first impression of Lourdes is bizarre. Hundreds of hotels, each foyer filled with wheelchairs and stretchers. Souvenir shops intersperse hotels; nuns, pushing patients, circumnavigate tourists of all nationalities. No evidence of depression anywhere in the town; helpers and sick appear to be enjoying themselves immensely. In the middle of all the dedicated activity, the river flows unperturbed. I circle the back streets until I find a fairly quiet hotel. Too late I discover it's home to a hundred young helpers and four priests from Northern Ireland.

It's the Crumlin, in Down and Connor, Diocesan annual pilgrimage. The sick of the parish are flown straight to the hospital while the helpers, aged between 17 and 25, are brought by coach; travelling by night over unseen landscapes, stopping only for essential vomiting. On arrival, they're allocated patients to wheel, carry or walk to what their Time Table describes as "Anointing of the Sick…Penitential Service…Bartres Mass for Able-bodied Pilgrims…Picnic and Concert for Hospital Sick…"

'It's great crack,' Marie-Clare tells me. I feel slightly disconcerted at the idea of drug abuse on a Diocesan pilgrimage but it turns out I'm the only one who doesn't know "craic" is Irish for "fun". There's a long waiting list to join the team. 'We get two free T-shirts with the Down and Connor emblems and are on first name terms with the priests. I like the Mass here, everyone sings – at school Masses, nobody sings.' Marie-Clare is just 17 and loving every minute. She's looking after Maureen, who's in her late thirties and has a heart problem. 'The healing baths are great,' Marie-Clare enthuses, 'but very cold. We have to leave our bras on but not our knickers.' She doesn't know why.

I'm invited to their last night party – 11.00p.m. at the café Jean D'Arc. There's time before the "craic" to take in the celebrated Torchlight Procession and International Mass and, of course, the Grotto. I put on my Jesus-throwing-the-merchants-out-of-the-temple hat but my cynicism is melted by the sincerity and respect I can see and tangibly feel as thousands of pilgrims move slowly, singing, towards the basilica. Stretcher cases make up the first few rows and then those who can't stand. The white of nun's and nurse's uniforms sparkle up and down the rows. Far back, amongst the tourists and seemingly able-bodied, I pass a beautiful young Indian woman in a wheelchair; her long black hair covers a baby that she rocks to the sweet singing. A six-foot, swarthy priest wheels a young man so broken in body, he can't lift head or hand. I watch the giant priest tenderly stroke the lolling head and feel rather than see a pleased response. And yes, it does hurt to see so much pain. I thought I wouldn't be able to bear the raised hopes and eager expectations because, statistically, there have been very few cures at Lourdes. I found, instead, a quiet faith; a spirit of love and care in the simple enjoyment of participation.

At the Grotto, a sign flashes in six languages the date of St B's vision and the Uriah Heepish English translation of the Virgin's request: 'Would you do me the favour of coming here for the next 15 days.' You can only go through the Grotto itself one at a time but people are sitting quietly, some kneeling on the ground, mostly praying. Chattering is discouraged by an occasional incongruous "Ssh!" over the loudspeaker, like an irritable teacher admonishing children at Assembly. The atmosphere is so reverential that it's a shock when a stout woman pushes her way roughly through the pilgrim file, followed by a small embarrassed man. On reaching the grotto, she poses for a photo and then marches out again. One rather hopes she'd choke on the Holy Water and be obliged to return to the Grotto in a humbler frame of mind and body. On that uncharitable thought, it's my turn to enter the Grotto and, touching the wall of the cave where it all happened, I'm thankfully surprised I haven't turned into a frog.

At 11.00p.m. the bar at the Café jean D'Arc, upstairs and overlooking the river, is packed with helpers of all nationalities competing loudly in song. It soon becomes clear that there's going to be trouble between the beautiful bronze and bejewelled Italian male contingent – who are avidly chatting up the Irish girls – and the red-faced pimply but decidedly more robust Irish lads. The songs become more aggressive – with graphic gestures – as the beer flows, until an Italian brings it to a head by standing up and kissing a red-haired Irish lovely in a long lingering clinch to the clapping and cheers of his friends. Fortunately, at that moment, the Scottish contingent step in to back their Gaelic brothers and the Italians make a wide retreat to the other side of the river where the vocal taunting continues on both sides. 'We're not allowed to go out with non-English speaking guys,' Marie-Clare giggles. At 3.00a.m. I manage to escape back to the momentarily silent hotel.

As there was no actual violence – due, I've no doubt, to the intervention of the blessed Saint Bernadette – it was quite entertaining and preferable to the English contingent of helpers who gathered in another bar I chanced upon prior to the Jean D'Arc. From the Diocese of Amplethorpe, ex-Amp. Public School, they were yuckishly yuppy. Young women with hard, horsey faces; everyone braying loudly in mutual admiration over their warm champagne. Sitting at the same table, I was ignored with the same totality as the Connor crowd had accepted me. However, they do pay all their own expenses – a week with flight cost them £400 a head. I'll certainly not throw the first stone. Nor, maybe, the last.

Serendipitying my way back through the Haut-Garonne towards Spain, I come across a small, walled mountain village: Saint Bertrand de Comminges. Perched on a steep stone incline above the Auberge is an 11th century cathedral where tonight - for–one night only – the Russian Patriarchate Choir will be singing *La Divine Liturgie des Sants Pierre et Paul*. Half an hour before the concert is due to start, the Pyrenean Princess has a tantrum that shakes the old inn's walls and then sobs her heart out with torrential rain. The Auberge is opposite the cathedral but it's a very wet walk up the steep incline. Lightning and thunder show up the medieval building like Frankenstein's castle. It's a fitting background for the ten monks walking slowly to the altar. Pony-tailed, bearded, Slavic features accentuated by long black habits, they look as romantic as Rasputin on a particularly good day. Standing in a semi-circle, their eyes fixed on the conductor, the plainsong transcends fantasy.

Their whole beings, although taught with concentration to get each note perfect, hold a stress-free serenity that expresses a spiritual as well as musical harmony. *La Divine Liturgie des saints Pierre et Paul* was indeed divine.

It's downhill all the way back to Spain. I move, imperceptibly, from the Haut Pyrenne to the Alt Pirineo. At the end of the Pass I stop for coffee and petrol – at a third of the French price. Viva España! Vive la difference!

CHAPTER FIFTEEN – NIGHTLY GALES AND NIGHTINGALES

I love Cantabria: lush, green, eat-your-heart-out-Julie Andrews hills, dotted – yes, dotted – with Swiss chalet style houses, rust coloured roofs on cream. Out of season, even honey pots such as Castro Urdiales and Santillana del Mar are enjoyable. The Santander-Bilbao motorway cuts through the mountains cleanly. Turning off on to the smaller coastal road means switching centuries. In February, solitary men scythe their meadows, piling the grass on to horse-drawn carts and then resting on top, while the horse makes its own way back home for dinner. There's a village called Hoja, on the way to Castro Urdiales. This is where the Spanish settled after making their fortunes in 19th century America. Giant palm trees box in the palatial orange houses standing in ornate gardens but there's a feeling of rust about them. Some seem inhabited, some left for dead.

In Castro, I get my car parked for the price of a drink at Meson Manero. It boasts the best of Cantabrian cuisine. A tableau of fish laid out like a celestial still life; wholesome, mouth-watering tapas. But it's too early for lunch and I drive up to the church sited spectacularly above the working harbour. "The finest Gothic structure in all Cantabria" my guidebook says. It's closed. There's a definite feeling of off-season in the litter strewn, seedy tenements, and washing hung cobbled streets.

Santillana del Mar is more tourist geared. There's hardly a corner in its arcaded plazas and bronzed mansions not sporting souvenirs but at the Parador I can take as much time as I like over a jug of sangria and exquisite potato croquettes in the sun-filled conservatory.

On a day of gale force winds and enough rain to ensure Cantabria's greenery for the foreseeable future, I discover Isla Playa. There's nothing especially Spanish about this tiny resort but it boasts a four-star hotel with the nicest manager I've ever come across. Hotel Olimpo was built in 1990. It's light, spacious and local artists cover the walls with paintings. Each June, there's an exhibition and one painting from each artist is chosen. The dining room is large and imposing. Made to cater for the Santander and Bilbao Sunday lunchers and 120 weddings and First Communions a year, it's empty on a winter weekday. The *menu del dia* is uninspiring but as it says in the hotel brochure's English translation: "It's not over weening to state…" that the á la carte and wine list excel.

Isla village above the playa has a Renaissance church and unswept bar opposite, where locals mix their home grown Moscatel type wine into unlabelled bottles. I know this because, dying for a pee, I go in and order a coffee. The place doubles as the village shop and I sit, knee deep in cigarette butts, surrounded by packets of sugar and tins of beans. Everyone stops talking to begin the well-known Spanish game of synchronised staring. Deciding that it would be more palatable to pee behind the wall in the churchyard, I brave the wet wind and cross the road. Too late I remember the old adage about wind and wetness. Stone angels synchronise disapproving stares as, uncomfortable but unrepentant, I make my way back to the car.

The huge car park on the playa warns of the summer invasion but now there's a pristine peacefulness about the cove and its empty apartments, as if the owners have left it in the immaculate hands of a loving housekeeper.

I first discover that Santander didn't belong to Brittany ferries when I actually stayed there. The ship I wanted to book for the return to Portsmouth was being thrashed by the wind and wet with a potential delay of ten hours. It seemed a better idea to stay and see the city. That's how I found Hotel las Brisas. The small door jammed between two bars is unpromising, but upstairs it's furnished like an upmarket Country House hotel. Except for the pictures, which are so Spanish naff, I have to ask about them. The owner reveals that he buys them in London's East-End markets. He worked as a London waiter in the sixties and made friends with a Spanish guy who now owns a button factory there and always tells him where to go for the best bargain. The red roses mounted in elaborate black and gold were bought for £25 in Liverpool Street.

You need to be street-wise in Santander. There's no place or time to map-read while you're in transit. I speak from tedious experience. The worst was trying to find a fun restaurant recommended by the pretty hotel receptionist. She gave me a map which I pretended to understand. So did half the population of Santander when I stopped to ask the way. A cold February night didn't prevent them from being bright and friendly before sending me off in differing directions. Finally, fate put a stop to the abortive merry-go-round when I found myself trapped at the end of a very long street. Cars parked nose to tail on both sides allowed a couple of paint-scratching inches to pass. But when the cars stopped, so did the street – nothing but a brick wall and a flight of narrow steps. No room to turn round, just an excruciatingly slow reverse back.

If there's one thing I know, but still haven't learnt, about Spain, it's the – shall we say – surprises of the street systems. I wouldn't mind if there was some consistency to the inconsistency. Modern Spain has evolved so quickly that it's not had time to catch up with itself. A native of southern Spain told me that there was logic to the wide tarmac roads that hairpin down to the coast. Before the motorcar, there was the donkey. The peasant, dozing comfortably on the donkey, allowed it to make its own energy-efficient way down to the sea. The tracks became well-trodden and, thereby, legitimate. Surveyors and such like costing money, it seemed economically viable to simply pour tarmac over the tracks.

I find that reasonably convincing but it still begs the question of why wide roads narrow to nothing at all or narrow roads end in brick walls. Or signs pointing optimistically to the "city centre" of a small town leave you at a junction that points to Madrid. Or the main road out of town is closed for the market necessitating a detour of three villages…Some suggest it's the Spanish psyche, but I'm not convinced – after all, the Romans were Latin. I bet they would have taken all the beggars off the streets of Santander and offered them 100% on what they normally make in a day to go round carving "Dead End" where applicable.

As it was, after the best part of an hour and a year's supply of patience, the need for fun evaporated. As dark as the night, I took my gloom back to the hotel. The café had closed and I finished up in bed with a packet of crisps and the TV, watching a Spanish singer whose lips and breasts would have brought the house down in Worksop Working Men's Club.

On that particular occasion, I sailed back to England the following day – the feast of St Valentine. Along with most of the poor Brits, who'd booked a romantic mini-cruise, I spent the entire day throwing up.

Most of old Santander was written off in 1941, which is when Santander began evolving into a resort. The Spanish come up for coolness from southern summers. On winter Sundays, the prosperous citizens parade on the prom – mamas competing for the furriest fur coat, papas evading coronaries with smug smiles.

An hour from Santander, 11km southeast of Cangas in a northerly sierra of the Picos Europa, is the religious shrine of Covadonga. It's startling to come across the Basilica – a Neo-Romanesque pink Victorian – attempting to compete in grandeur with the granite heights of the Picos. Strangely, the contrast works. At least it does on a weekday in late March when the tourists are minimal. I stay at the Hotel Pelayo, another Victorian edifice. It's like the Grand Hotels used to be in English resorts, but the garden of this hotel is a national park that's home to bears, wild boar, chamois, and even the occasional *asturcón* (wild horse). Spain has more birds of prey than any country in Europe. At Covadonga they sail and swoop –not, I hope, in search of tasty tourist tapas.

But this is a holy place – sacrosanct from predators- or so an English translation leaflet picked up at the tiny wooden booth, which serves as the local tourist office, tells me. It quotes from Ambrosio de Morales' 16th century Holy Journey:

"On a hig mountain of stoped rock, which faces a deep valley to which one arrives by a narrow, rough path, nature has formed a cave with deep capacity having graced it, with a little diligence, to some use: in it has been placed for ever the holy image of the Virgin Mary, our Lady."

I can't say I noticed any higs or stopes but the cave does contain the tomb of Don Pelayo – the guy who made it all possible by initiating the *Reconquista*. He set out from the cave in AD722 with his army and "the confidence of Christ" to rebut the Moors. The "confidence" was not misplaced - an avalanche destroyed the Muslim invasion. Although it took another 14 centuries for the ethnic cleansing to be completed, Covadonga remained the pivot of pilgrimage, in theory if not in practice. The poverty of the area and the difficult access precipitated a decline until the "monumental temple" was built in the 19th century. In 1918 the area was declared a Parque Nacional in honour of "the moment in which we consider Spain to have been conceived."

There's a tiny chapel in the cave where Santa Maria nestles. Parterres of Box lead from the cave to the church. In the middle is a fountain that is reputed to have magical qualities - married women would drink from it if they fancied a change of husband. A clever bit of marketing, perhaps, to increase the influx of female pilgrims.

In the unusually warm early evening the mountain mists descend and the huge granite statue of Pelayo, enveloped by darkening greenery, keeps company with eagles. The Victorian gas lamps light up; the shrubs of rosemary smell as intense as incense; the church bells sound the passing of time; nightingales begin their night long vigilance; a brown robed priest wanders out, fingers and lips caught up in catechism. There's a tangible feeling of holiness. Difficult to equate the savage violence of the Reconquest with this place "where God seeks man and where man may find Him." Maybe it's something to do with the higs and stopes.

Easter is the big exeunt in Spain. Everybody changes places, the northerners rush to the coast and the *Madrileños* accelerate two hours out of the city in all directions. It's not the best of times to be foot-loose and fancy free, so I make my way towards Potes in search of a rental before the Easter rush. On the way I succumb to the temptation of a free night at the Parador of Fuente Dé. (Two nights for the price of one with "Friends of Paradores".) Cantabria in March can be wet and cold as an English winter or as warm as a good May – the days and the area are microclimates. As I drive below the Macizo Oriental snow-capped peaks towards the dead end of Fuente Dé, it's difficult to imagine the traffic grid that takes place in summer as the day trippers make for the chair-lift that will swing them up 900m to the peaks – after a two-hour queue. Now the *teleférico* doesn't seem to be functioning at all. A few rain-soaked Spanish families wander round its base disconsolately before wisely enjoying the flower-filled woods instead.

Monday is market day at Potes and the Brittany Ferry brigade is enjoying every moment of the rainless respite. I manage to find a sort of travel agent who, after making some phone calls, tells me of the perfect place to rent for the nine days of Holy Week. I follow his flashy car up tracks that would have made a mule hesitate and there it is, a restored timbered fina style complex with six well-furnished attractive apartments, central heating, open fires with free wood, and flowers everywhere. I sit in the sun on my doorstep eating a fruit lunch and contemplating nine days of paradise. Suddenly a truck drives up and five minutes later it begins: hammering, sawing, drilling. I HAD asked the agent if it was very quiet and, of course, to him and every other Spaniard, it was.

And so I succumb to another Parador, at Cervera de Pisuerga. I know I'll get in because up to Easter they accept half-price tokens. It's a beautiful drive through green, flower-decked mountains that gradually give way to bleak moorland. I have the road to myself and arrive at the Parador at 7.00p.m. A magnificent building in a magnificent setting. I pay a supplement to enjoy a *matrimonial* (double bed) and a double aspect vista over mountain and lake. The sun's setting over the lake as I sip my *amigo* free drink of quite acceptable local wine.

During the night, the temperature drops and by mid-morning it's very cold with strong winds and heavy rain. Understandably, the Parador is loth to heat up its elegant lounge – the size of a suburban garden – for the very few visitors. There's nothing for it but to have lunch in the equally elegant restaurant. The Paradors excel at location and interior design but generally, fail on the food. Cervera de Pisuerga is an exception: fresh river trout with prune sauce, marinated boar, plus the customary freebie tapas and a jug of local red wine.

The rain continues and in the night the wind increases with alarming velocity. Shutters and balcony doors crash and the central heating, unable to bring the room up to any degree of warmth, moans its own loud grievances.

'June,' the receptionist tells me, when I hand in my key the next morning, 'you can be sure of good weather in June.' The Parador is full for Holy Week. I hope the guests bring their thermals.

The biting wind stays with me as I drive through the Cantabrian mountains on April Fool's Day. Bleak moors, sparse mining villages – you could be in Yorkshire. Perhaps that's the joke. The road to Santander descends rapidly towards the sea. It's like going from a black and white film to full technicolour. I'll try my luck at Isla Playa. Brittany Ferry Brits on Easter leave may well invade it but I very much doubt there'll be any higs and stopes.

CHAPTER SIXTEEN – THE FINAL FRONTIER

It's at St-Jean-Pied-de-Port in France that the blue and yellow signs first attract me. I'm almost out of pesetas and petrol but it seems an irresistible adventure: Santiago de Compostela, the third holiest site in Christendom after Jerusalem and Rome. And so I begin the Pilgrim's Way.

"After you, all the peoples will go on pilgrimage until the end of the centuries." This prophesy, made to Charlemagne in a dream by the Apostle James, appears to be factually – if ungrammatically – correct. The Camino de Santiago, known by its pilgrims as El Camino, is 450 miles long if you begin, as I did, on the watershed of the Pyrenees above Roncesvalles. According to the *Chanson de Rolan*, this is the site of the legendary eighth century battle between the Saracens and Charlemagne's previously undefeated army. As good a reason as any for a pilgrimage, I suppose.

Luzaide-Valcarlos, just across the border on the Ibañeta mountain Pass has a Casa Rural run by Isabel Iturriria Arnis. No ensuite bedrooms but everything is spotless and attractively traditional. The village bank is closed. I've got just enough pesetas to pay for the room but not enough for dinner. There's a shop but it doesn't take credit cards. A night of fasting – forlornly appropriate before the onset of the pilgrimage. The young hostess thinks differently and invites me into her kitchen to share a bottle of *Rosado,* potted cheese, Serano ham and bread. She's glad of the company. Her husband works all week in a metal factory 40 miles away. He comes home at weekends and helps her in the work. She's a trained chef – at one-time cooking for the Spanish president – and when the Casa is full in high season, makes dinner for 14 guests each night. I pick my way laboriously through conversation in little bite size tapas of French, English and Spanish until the early hours of the morning.

It's easy enough to get petrol and pesetas the next morning in Roncesvalles, where three of the four pilgrim routes from France meet up. The geographical position of Santiago de Compostela on the western edge of the Pyrenees makes this route convenient for thousands of European pilgrims. Roncesvalles also has the first work of classical Gothic architecture imported from France to Spain: The Collegiate church of Santa Maria de Orreaga-Roncesvalles, burial place of large numbers of pilgrims. I don't go and see it. Why? Because if I'm going to make it to Santiago in seven days – as my budget dictates – I'm going to have to prioritise. (It's not entirely unprecedented, Dante's visionary journey in his masterpiece, The Divine Comedy, takes only one week.)

EN ROUTE

Since the beginning of the ninth century, when the bones of the Apostle were placed in the specially built basilica at Santiago de Compostela, pilgrims have proliferated. At the height of its popularity in the 11th and 12th centuries, a traveller, one Emir ben Yussuf, complained "the multitude of pilgrims on their way to Compostela or their way back is so great that there is hardly any roadway free to travel west." The trouble was compounded by so many artists and craftsmen amongst the pilgrims wanting to stop en route to participate in the construction of hospitals, churches and hermitages, encouraged, of course, by the local tourist boards. 800 years later, even the most fanatical art historian would be sated with sacred edifices and would require at least one whole day per 20 miles to even scrape the surface. Art appreciation was not on the agenda for the earliest pilgrims. I'm going to try and do it their Way. Pilgrimage is a movement of the mind's perspective –unpredictable. Cut loose and hang loose.

The road through Navarra in Spring is so alluring, with bright red poppies mingling in the banks of yellow flowers, that it's easy to keep going with only hilltop hermitages and low flying storks for company. On the third day, Sunday, I'm tootling through Rioja Alta to San Martin de Cogolla. Coming through landscape that makes it easy to contemplate the Divine, the Monasterio de San Millán appears on the horizon like the dwelling place of God. I don't know that it's a four-star hotel and drive into the deserted dusty village. There doesn't seem to be anywhere to stay. In desperation,

I ask a woman sweeping the road outside her house. *'Momentito,'* she replies, and disappears up a side street into a building. I don't know what's happening and know even less when another woman appears in a dressing gown and slippers. She smiles and beckons, so I follow her, hopefully, down the street until she indicates that I should park the car. Unlocking the door of a terraced house, she motions me to follow. My expectations lower with every step I climb. How am I going to get out of this one? And where am I going to find somewhere better? But the apartment is brand new and adequately furnished. Her husband is a builder and has renovated the house in his spare time. I can have it for 3000pts a day. She works as a chambermaid at the Hosteria del Monasterio de San Millán. Have dinner there tonight, she suggests. Shall I pay you now? No, bring the money up to the hotel before you leave in the morning. No name, no address, no passport: trusted pilgrims!

The hotel is in one wing of the 16th century monastery. The first books in Castillano are here – one of the monks wrote in this language as he jotted notes beside the Latin religious text. The huge cobbled plaza outside the San Millán also includes the Monasterio de Yuso and a small building, recently opened by the King and Queen of Spain, devoted to the Castillian language. The buildings are not open so I settle for dinner at the historic hotel. Sunday evening is rarely a sociable time to eat in a country where Sunday lunch is the pivot of the week. There are no other diners and no staff. I am waited on personally and pleasurably by the hotel manageress.

Burgos, "Head of Castile," is the next stop. I've bypassed it many times on my way to the Santander ferry. Now I have an excuse to go into the city and visit the cathedral. For the car-less pilgrims, walking into Spanish cities must be a nightmare trek through miles of factories, warehouses, garages and hideous high-rises. Only the fanatic footers will refuse to bus it. But the cathedral is magnificent. A fellow pilgrim points out the genius of the craftsmen – they could do as well as Goya but in three-dimensional stone and for storing outdoors. Why don't they have a bench, he grumbles, you could spend days perusing such genius. I don't have days and I expect a bench would be taken up permanently by the beggars that line the steps outside. In defiance of the church authorities I watch the pilgrim give a generous donation to a pretty, smartly dressed girl who is holding out an empty shoebox. Well, who am I to deny her another pair of Gucci's?

I arrive at Santo Domingo de la Calzada. Another cobbled plaza with another historic building, built in 1216 as a hostel for pilgrims who were glad of a straw mattress, crude wine and bread. Now it's a Parador and pilgrims have to make do with stately living rooms, elegant en-suite bedrooms and a dinner of sufficient quality to accompany the world-renowned wines of Rioja. I compromise with a picnic in my room to subsidise the cost of the room.

Next to the "hospital" is a cathedral with an amazing sarcophagus containing the remains of Saint Domingo – a man with an amazing story. A hermit, he lived in a deserted wood on the site of Calzada at the end of the 11th century. Seeing the labours of the pilgrims, he built a 24-span bridge to help them over the tortuous terrain, and then set up lodgings and hospital where he looked after them. In 1098, the King made him a gift of a site near the construction of a church and laid the first stone himself. It was consecrated in 1106 but the saintly saint didn't want to be buried in what was to become a cathedral. He built himself a humble tomb alongside the church and the road he had built.

But why, the passing pilgrim might ask, is there a live white cockerel and hen in a cage above the sarcophagus? The answer, my friend, is in a document dating from 1350 in the cathedral archive. The story goes like this:

Among the many pilgrims on their way to Santiago who stopped to venerate the reliquaries of Santo Domingo, was a married couple from Cologne with their 18-year-old son, Hugonell. The girl at the inn where they lodged fell in love with Hugonell but, ignored, she decided to take her revenge. She put a silver cup in his luggage and when they left, she denounced him for the robbery. The laws of the time punished robbery with death and the innocent pilgrim was hanged. Before continuing their journey to Santiago, the parents paid a last visit to their hanged offspring. As they arrived they heard his voice telling them that Saint Domingo had saved his life. They immediately rushed to police Headquarters to tell the chief about the miracle. He was sitting down to lunch and sneered at them that their son was about as alive as the roast cock and hen he was about to eat. At that very moment, the cock and hen became covered in feathers and leaped from the plate, crowing and clucking. In memory of this event, a live cock and hen, always white, are kept throughout the year in the cathedral. They are donated and changed each month.

I didn't hear the cockerel crow from its gilded cage, but most of the day and night the plaza vibrates with awesome tolling. Sonorous, laboured and discordant bells slowly pick their way through misery and loss. A disconcerting experience.

Back on route, weather and scenery vary from place to place, day to day, almost moment to moment; but the churches and monasteries provide a consistency that gives the impression of not moving at all. Sometimes the blue and yellow signs take me along lorry-laden roads – a proper penance for the poor pilgrims inhaling black diesel fumes; but at other times the roles are reversed as I bump through muck-filled farmyards, discarded hovels lining the neglected road, watching the pilgrims strolling through mountain paths knee-high in wild flowers and herbs. Now and then I come across a great pile of stones where pilgrims have left tokens of flowers or crosses. The genuine pilgrim has to produce a letter from his parish priest in order to obtain credentials entitling him to use the hospices on The Way. Not having such credentials I'm obliged to utilise a higher echelon where I can get a room with a loo – if not a view.

Hotel Royal Monasterio de Santo Zolio in Palencia has rooms with loos and views, it's been a lodging house since 947 as a monastery for Benedictines, then Cluniacs and finally, from the mid-19ᵗʰ century until 1956, Jesuits. It's still only partially restored; there's no one around to mind if you wander through the passages and look down on the original old chapel festering in spiders and rotten wood. Now the monastery returns to being a stop-over for kings and pilgrims alike. Both would be at home here in its stylish simplicity and silent solitude. Somewhere along The Way, I've learnt about 12ᵗʰ century French monk, Aymery Picaud, who wrote the first "How To" book on El Camino, called the Codex Calixtino. He tells of the hospitals having bells, which rang during the night and on foggy days to guide pilgrims who might have lost their way. The Royal Monasterio de Santo Zolio rang no bells so it's strange that I found it, off the route and without a guide book. Unless, of course, you believe in angels.

I meet up now and then with English pilgrims, including a couple in their seventies from north of Berwick on Tweed, the man resplendent in kilt and sporran like an antiquated Braveheart; and two show-biz guys who walk two weeks of The Way each year and suffer the occasional intimidating interviews with austere abbots who remain unconvinced that they are Protestants by default and haven't the least intention of seducing nuns – or priests – en route.

At last I'm in Leon, described in the Codex Calixtino as being "Royal and Curial, filled with all sorts of happiness." There are two things I have to see here. One is the cathedral of Santa Maria – the Chartres of Spain – and the other is the Mionasterio-Hospital del San Marcos. This "monumental building featuring a Plateresque façade built around 1515, conceals an interior filled with works of art." I shuffle in amongst other pilgrims who are not too proud to spend another night at a Parador. The interior of the cathedral is a prodigy of light and glass. It's all a bit too much for me. I'm beginning to feel like the stone statue of the pilgrim Santiago, standing forlornly on the main front, worn away with the kisses of pilgrims – only I'm worn away with seeing stone statues. I can see how visual artists relish the statuary of cathedral and cloister, their meditations heightened by the skill of stone-masons. I, the Philistine, become bored and usually come away cold in body and emotion. I'm partially revived by a quaint little booklet issued by the tourist office:

"Come to the Path of Santiago and get to know us. We have been so many years as wayfarers along this path that you will never catch us asleep like the foolish Virgins of the Gospel; our oil bottle nourished with the best oil that we have, will enlighten your steps in this gentle land of yesteryear, which with hearts bursting with hope for the pardon of sins or in a happy adventure, men and women would flock from all over Europe and you will discover, precisely on the millennium that in a twinkling of an eye is about to take its leave, all that we have been left; the best of all no doubt being the warm welcome that all traveller receives."

I've got enough Parador points for a free night at the Parador Villafranca del Bierzo on the last leg of the journey, turning off the main road following the old Pilgrim's Way through Montes de Leon. It's early evening and for two hours I see no other car, just moorland and wild flowers of yellow, blue and purple that change colour as the dark mists close in. Only the white broom remains unchallenged by the encroaching night.

Villafranca del Bierzo with its surrealistic min-mountains of coal is a shock after the magical moors. A reminder to the pilgrim that he is approaching the region known in early times as Finis Terrae, because it was the western limit of the then known world. The city of Santiago de Compostello was thought to bring together a geographical and theological idea of the end or usefulness of life. The Parador, minimal and mediocre, does nothing to dispel this idea but, frankly, I'm too tired to care.

And so I arrive at Santiago de Compostello. The city shines in the afternoon sunlight – a miracle in itself. Situated in the wettest fold of the Gallego hills, it enjoys three times more rainfall than London or Paris. Cars are banned from the enormous space of the Praza de Obarorio, another cobbled plaza, dominated by the cathedral and the Hostal de los Reyes Católicos. But I park anyway. The Hostal is, surprise, surprise, a Parador. More surprising is that at the equivalent of £140 a night, it's full. I don't think I would have been tempted – it's as over budget for me as it was for King Ferdinand and Queen Isabella. They commissioned the hospice in gratitude for their victory at Granada, which finally put paid to the Muslim invasion. The people of Compostello who had to finance the construction didn't share their gratitude; nor did the farmers who were thrown off the site without compensation; nor did the mayor who had to provide free board and lodging for the hordes of workmen. However, everyone decided it was well worth it in the end and things settled down for 450 years when, in 1954, more money was dished out – by the government this time, a cool six million pounds – to convert it into a five-star hotel.

Sitting in one of its impressive arcaded patios (preferable to the vaulted crypt bar, where the bodies of dead pilgrims were stored) enjoying a china jug of Sangria – and with one eye on the policeman strolling by the Beema – I can admire the exterior of the cathedral, described by Jan Morris as "unquestionably one of the great buildings of the world." While tourists and pilgrims pay homage to the imposing edifice, students from the university, in medieval garb, pay their fees with flute and guitar, adding a welcome touch of life and reality.

I find a comfortable cloister for the night at the Hostal-Hogar San Francisco, a "hospital" founded by St Francis of Assisi. Brown-gowned Friars wander silently through chattering tourists who seem more intent on their stomachs than their souls. The coach has agitated them away by the time I get up, over-tired and over-stretched, to make my way to the cathedral for the culmination of my journey – the Pilgrim's Mass. In the cathedral, behind the Chancel, dark steep steps and a cold narrow passage lead past the golden sepulchre containing the bones of the Apostle James. It's surprisingly moving; as if by looking at the bones of the man who walked by the side of Christ, one is touching Christ himself.

There's time to sit in a pew and reflect before the Mass begins. More on the state of my feet, I feel, than on the state of my soul – which seems in comparison to be quite sprightly. I haven't the excuse of the bona fide pilgrims who've walked or cycled the 500 miles and earned the right to eat in the Parador's staff canteen, receive their *Compostello* certification and return, with pride, to hang up their tattered shoes in church.

On further reflection, it's not my feet that ache but my eyes. There's been an over-indulgence of interest, a surfeit of stone, almost a hallucination of history and certainly a surplus of scenery. No, it's not my eyes – it's the eyes of my mind. It's exactly what Walter Starkie wrote in The Road to Santiago: "A reflective pilgrim on the road to Santiago always makes a double journey…the backward journey through Time and the forward journey through Space…every step evokes memories of those who passed that way century after century."

Perhaps it's that presence I can feel now. There's a charge in the air that makes my blood flow a little faster as if James, the son of Zebedee, had left not just his bones in the golden sepulchre but something intangible that excites the spiritual perception. It's easy to be cynical about walking 500 miles to see a load of hidden bones; harder perhaps, to understand and accept that 2000 years after three pilgrims followed a star to kneel before a symbol of truth, there are men and women with the same idea.

You can see by the expression on the faces of the pilgrims that for them it's not a formality at the end of a very long walk but a mystical experience – perhaps like touching the hand of God at the end of a very long search for reality. If travel broadens the mind, then it's not inconceivable that travel with a spiritual purpose clarifies identity.

My little tourist booklet from Leon tells me that at the village of Foncebadón, the last stage of El Camino in Castilla y Leon, pilgrims can chant "the good luck of belonging to the pilgrim life with no other occupation, with no other name and with no other village."

Outside the cathedral, the rain has begun again. The wet roads shine invitingly into Galicia and on to – anywhere you like. El Camino need not stop at Santiago de Compostello. I don't know what the future will bring but at the moment I have no other occupation, no other village, and perhaps Pilgrim is as good a name as any other.

ENDS

Lightning Source UK Ltd.
Milton Keynes UK
UKRC01n1839310118
317153UK00003B/12